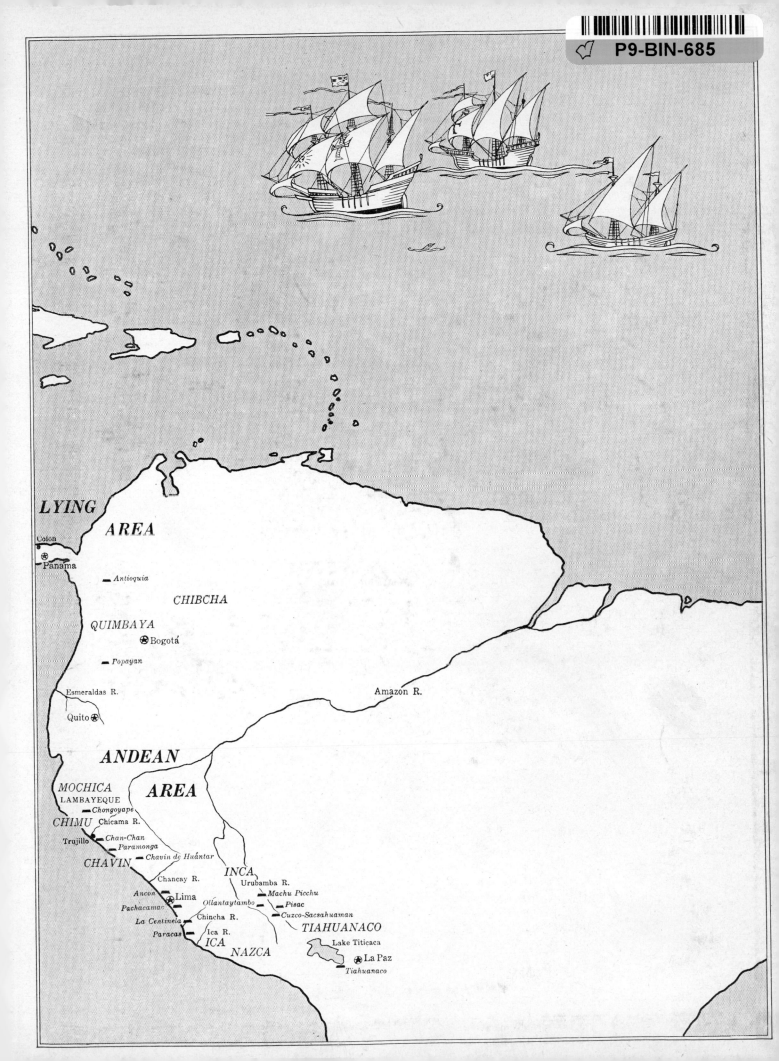

*LYING*

*AREA*

Colon
⊛ Panama

— *Antioquia*

*CHIBCHA*

*QUIMBAYA*
⊛ Bogotá

— *Popayan*

Esmeraldas R.

Amazon R.

Quito ⊛

*ANDEAN*

*MOCHICA*
LAMBAYEQUE                *AREA*
— *Chongoyape*
*CHIMU*  Chicama R.
— *Chan-Chan*
Trujillo  — *Paramonga*
— *Chavin de Huántar*
*CHAVIN*
Chancay R.        *INCA*
Urubamba R.
*Ancon* —        — *Machu Picchu*
Pachacamac  ⊛ Lima  *Ollantaytambo*  — *Pisac*
La Centinela — Chincha R.  — *Cuzco-Sacsahuaman*
*Paracas* —        *TIAHUANACO*
Ica R.
*ICA*  *NAZCA*  Lake Titicaca
⊛ La Paz
*Tiahuanaco*

# MEDIEVAL AMERICAN ART

# MEDIEVAL AMERICAN ART

## A SURVEY IN TWO VOLUMES

by

## PÁL KELEMEN

VOLUME II

## THE MACMILLAN COMPANY

NEW YORK · 1946

# Contents

VOLUME II

ILLUSTRATIONS

Much of the material in this volume has never before been published and in certain instances permission to use the illustrations was given only reluctantly. For this reason special attention is called to the copyright © of this survey.

# ARCHITECTURE

*a*

*b*

PLATE I.  ©.  *a*) Rito de los Frijoles, New Mexico.  Talus-houses, with community dwelling in the foreground.  *b*) Mesa Verde, Colorado.  Spruce Tree House.

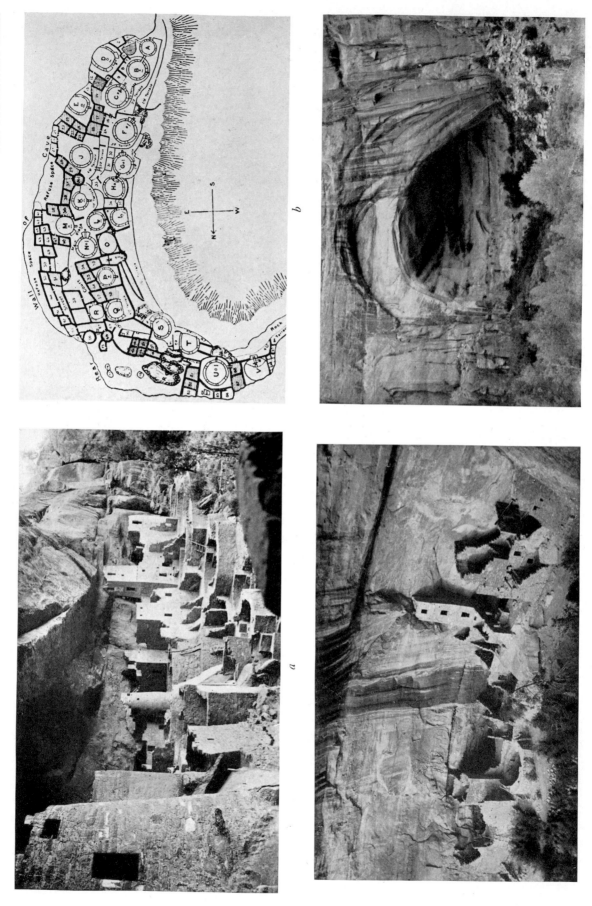

PLATE 2. ©. *a* and *c*) Mesa Verde, Colorado. Cliff Palace and Square Tower House. *b*) Ground plan of Cliff Palace. *d*) Betatakin Ruin, Navaho National Monument, Arizona.

PLATE 3.  ©.  Canyon de Chelly, Arizona.  White House.

*a*

*b*

PLATE. 4  ©.  Pueblo Bonito, Chaco Canyon, New Mexico.  *a*) View from rear.  *b*) Theoretical
reconstruction.  View from front.

*a*

*b*

PLATE 5.   ©.   *a*) Chetro Ketl, Chaco Canyon, New Mexico.   Great kiva.   *b*) Aztec Ruin, New Mexico.
Interior of reconstructed kiva.

*a*

*b*

PLATE 6.  ©.  *a*) Walpi, Arizona.  A Hopi village.  *b*) Taos, New Mexico.  Five-story community dwelling.

*a*

*b*

PLATE 7.  ©.  Teotihuacan, Mexico.  *a*) General view.  Inset: section of the Citadel.
*b*) Pyramid of the Sun.

*a*

*b*

PLATE 8.  ©.  Teotihuacan, Mexico.  *a*) Temple of Quetzalcoatl.  *b*) Detail.

*a*

*b*

PLATE 9. Ⓒ. Xochicalco, Mexico. *a*) Temple-base. *b*) Detail.

*b*

*d*

*a*

*c*

PLATE 10. ©. Malinalco, Mexico. *a*) Monolithic temple. *b*) Near view of entrance. *c*) Interior of temple. *d*) Calixtlahuaca, Mexico. Round temple-base.

*a*

*b*

*c*

PLATE 11.  ©.  Tenayuca, Mexico.  *a*) Temple-base.  *b*) Detail of early stairway.  *c*) Fire Serpent, with section of temple-base.

*a*

*b*

*c*

PLATE 12.  ©.  *a*) El Tajin, Papantla, Mexico.  *b*) Stairway.  *c*) Airview.

a

b

c

PLATE 13.   ©.   Monte Alban, Mexico.   *a*) View of the Great Plaza, looking north.   *b*) Archway, Monticle J.   *c*) Monticle M.

*a*

*b*

PLATE 14.   ©.   Monte Alban, Mexico.   *a*) View of the Great Plaza, looking south.   *b*) Ball Court.

PLATE 15.  ©.  Monte Alban, Mexico.  *a*) North end of the Temple of the Tiger.  *b*) Entrance to fabulous Tomb 7.  *c*) Entrance to Tomb 125.  *d*) Entrance to frescoed Tomb 104.

*a*

*b*

PLATE 16.   ©.   Mitla, Mexico.   *a*) Palace II.   *b*) View from southwest.

PLATE 17. ©. Mitla, Mexico. a) Profile of Palace II façade, looking west. b) Inner court. c) Inner chamber.

*a*

*b*

PLATE 18.  ©.  Mitla, Mexico.  *a*) Court of the Tombs, north section, showing tomb entrance.
*b*) Interior of east tomb.

*a*

*b*

PLATE 19.   ©.   Uaxactun, Guatemala.   *a*) Airview of temple-base (Structure E-VII).   *b*) Near view.

*b*

*d*

*a*

*c*

PLATE 20. ⓒ. Copan, Honduras. *a*) Great Plaza. *b*) Model of site. *c*) Reviewing Stand. *d*) Ball Court.

*a*

*b*

PLATE 21.  ©.  Copan, Honduras.  *a*) Hieroglyphic
Stairway.  *b*) Detail of balustrade.

*a*

*b*

PLATE 22.  ©  Copan, Honduras.  *a*) Temple of the Sculptured Doorway (Structure 22).
*b*) Entrance.

*a*                                                              *b*

*c*

PLATE 23.  ©.  Copan, Honduras.  Views of the sculptured doorway.

PLATE 24.  ©.  Tikal, Guatemala.  View from Temple I, looking toward temples II, III, and IV.

*a*

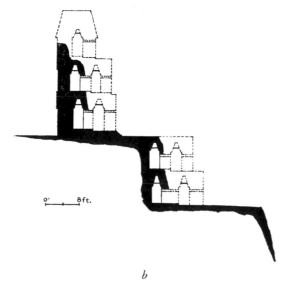

0'   8 ft.

*b*

PLATE 25. ©. Tikal, Guatemala. *a*) Rear section of the Palace of the Five Stories (Structure 10). *b*) Cross-section of same.

*a*

*b*

PLATE 26.  ©.  Palenque, Mexico.  *a*) General view of the Palace Group.  *b*) House A from court.

*a*

*b*

PLATE 27.  ©.  Palenque, Mexico.  *a*) Temple of the Cross.  Note the inner vaulting revealed by
the collapsed façade.  *b*) Model of theoretical reconstruction.

*a*

*b*

**PLATE 28.** ©. Rio Bec B, Mexico. *a*) Building 1. *b*) Model.

*a*

*b*

PLATE 29.   ⓒ.   Tulum, Mexico.   *a*) Castillo group, showing natural seawall.   *b*) Castillo viewed from court.

*a*

*b*

PLATE 30.   Ⓒ.   Tulum, Mexico.   *a*) Temple of the Frescoes.   *b*) Model.

*a*

*b*

PLATE 31.  ©.  *a*) Sayil, Mexico.  Palace.  *b*) Uaxactun, Guatemala.  Present-day house.

*a*

*b*

PLATE 32.  ⓒ.  Labná, Mexico.  *a*) Gateway.  *b*) Detail of Great Palace (Structure I).

*a*

*b*

*d*

*c*

PLATE 33. ©. Yucatan, Mexico. Flying façades: *a*) Structure XI, Labná; *b*) temple, Sabacche; *c*) Red House, Chichen Itzá; *d*) model of Red House, showing cross-section.

*a*

*b*

PLATE 34.  ⓒ.  Kabah, Mexico.  *a*) Palace I from southwest.  *b*) Detail.

*a*

*b*

PLATE 35.  ©.  Uxmal, Mexico.  *a*) Temple of the Dwarf and corner of the Nunnery.  *b*) Palace of
the Governor, House of the Turtles, House of the Doves.

*a*

*b*

*c*

PLATE 36. ©. Uxmal, Mexico. *a*) Façade of Palace of the Governor. *b* and *c*) Details, inner court of the Nunnery.

*a*

*b*

PLATE 37.   ©.   Uxmal, Mexico.   *a*) The Nunnery complex from the Palace of the Governor.   *b*) East
building of the Nunnery from the inner court.

*a*

*b*

PLATE 38.   ©.   Chichen Itzá, Mexico.   *a*) The Nunnery.   *b*) East end.

*a*

*b*

PLATE 39.   ©.   Chichen Itzá, Mexico.   *a*) The Observatory, or Caracol.   *b*) Temple of the Three Lintels.

*a*

*b*

PLATE 40.  ©.   Chichen Itzá, Mexico.  *a*) Temple of the Tigers.  *b*) Ball Court.

PLATE 41. ©. Chichen Itzá, Mexico. El Castillo.

*a*

*b*

PLATE 42.   ©. Chichen Itzá, Mexico.   *a*) Frontal view of the Temple of the Warriors.
*b*) Southwest corner of upper building.

*a*

*b*

PLATE 43.   ©.   Chan-Chan, Peru.   *a*) Walls with stucco-like decoration.   *b*) Hall of the Arabesques.

PLATE 44. © Paramonga, Peru. La Fortaleza.

*a*

*b*

PLATE 45.   Ⓒ.   *a*) La Centinela, Chincha Valley, Peru.   *b*) Adjoining palace.

*a*

*b*

PLATE 46.   ©.   Tiahuanaco, Bolivia.   *a*) Gateway of the Sun.   *b*) Detail.

*a*

*b*

PLATE 47.   ©.   *a*) Pirapi, Bolivia.   Burial towers, or *chulpas*.   *b*) Sillustani, Bolivia.   Burial tower.

*a*

*b*

PLATE 48.   ©.   *a*) Cuzco, Peru.   Street showing Inca masonry.   *b*) Ruins at Tampumachay, near Cuzco.

*a*

*b*

PLATE 49.  ©.  Sacsahuaman, Peru.  *a*) Fortress.  *b*) Throne of the Inca.

*a*

*b*

PLATE 50.   ©.   Ollantaytambo, Peru.   *a*) Ruins with fountain.   *b*) Hall of the Niches.

*a*

*b*

PLATE 51.   ©.   Pisac, Peru.   *a*) Semicircular ruins of "garrison."   *b*) Section of temple group.

*a*

*b*

PLATE 52.   ©.   Pisac, Peru.   *a*) Entrance to Sundial, or *Intihuatana*.   *b*) Rear view.

PLATE 53. ©. Machu Picchu, Peru. General view.

*a*

*b*

PLATE 54.   ©.   Machu Picchu, Peru.   *a*) Semicircular tower.   *b*) Ruins below great temple.

*a*

*b*

*c*

PLATE 55.   ©.   Machu Picchu, Peru.   *a*) Masonry combined with carved living rock.
*b*) Detail of tower.   *c*) View of tower.

*a*

*b*

PLATE 56.  ©.  Machu Picchu, Peru.  *a*) View of King's Group.  *b*) Ruins of terraces.

# SCULPTURE

*b*

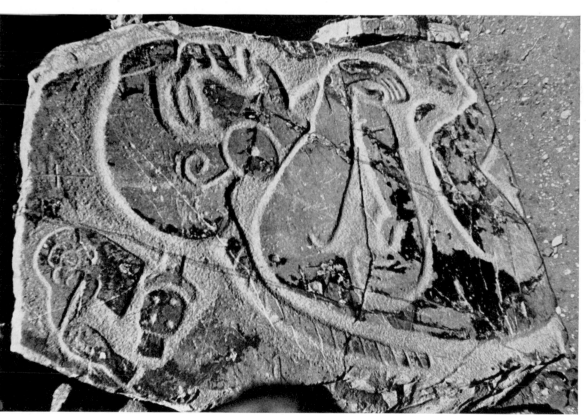

*a*

PLATE 57. ©. Sculptured stone slabs, Monte Alban, Mexico.

*a*

*b*

PLATE 58. ©. *a*) Zapotec stone relief. *b*) Aztec stone relief.

PLATE 59.  ©.  *a*) Huaxtec figure.  *b*) Aztec "pulque vessel."  *c*) Aztec Goddess of Agriculture.

*a*

*b*

*c*

PLATE 60.   ©.   Aztec animal figures:   *a*) rattlesnake;   *b*) toad;   *c*) "dog."

*a*

*b*

PLATE 61.  ©.  *a*) Aztec seated figure.  *b*) Recumbent anthropomorph, Vera Cruz?.

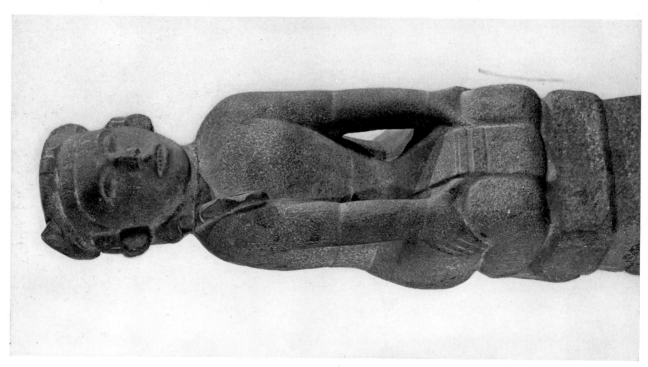

*a*

*b*

PLATE 62.  ©.  Two seated stone figures:  *a*) probably from Vera Cruz;  *b*) Aztec.

*a*

*b*                                                                 *c*

PLATE 63.  ©.  *a*) Stone relief from Ball Court, El Tajin, Papantla, Mexico.  *b*) Relief in fired clay, southern Mexico.  *c*) Eagle stone relief, Chichen Itzá, Mexico.

*a*

*b*

PLATE 64.   ©.   *a*) Totonac yoke.   *b*) Detail of one end.

*a*

*b*

*c*

PLATE 65.   ⓒ.   Details of three Totonac yokes.

*b*

*a*

PLATE 66. ©. Two Totonac axe-shaped stone heads.

PLATE 67.  ©.  Three Totonac *palmas*.

*a*

*b*

*c*

*a*

*b*

*c*

*d*

PLATE 68.  ©.  Four sculptured stone heads from Mexico.

PLATE 69. ©. *a*) Totonac stela, Tepetlaxco, Mexico. *b*) Carved stone disc, southeastern Mexico. *c*) Maya stela, Tenam, Mexico.

PLATE 70. ©. *a*) Stela 16, Tikal, Guatemala. *b*) Stela 10, Xultun, Guatemala.

*b*

*a*

*a*

*b*

*c*

PLATE 71. ©. *a*) Stela H, Copan, Honduras. *b* and *c*) Detail and north side of Stela D, Quiriguá, Guatemala.

PLATE 72. ©. *a* and *b*) Stela 6 and Stela 14, Piedras Negras, Guatemala. *c*) Stela I, Quiriguá, Guatemala. Rear view.

*a*

*b*

*c*

*a*

*b*

PLATE 73.  ©.  *a*) Stela 40, Piedras Negras, Guatemala.  *b*) Detail of upper half.

*a*

*b*

PLATE 74.  ⓒ.  *a*) Stela 12, Piedras Negras, Guatemala.  *b*) Detail of lower third.

*c*

*b*

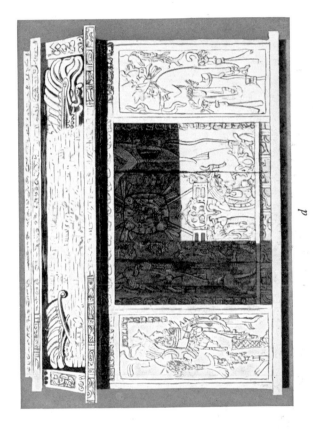

*d*

*a*

PLATE 75. ©. *a, b,* and *c*) Sculptured stone tablets from the sanctuary, Temple of the Sun, Palenque, Mexico. *d*) Drawing by F. Catherwood, showing their original position.

*b*

*a*

PLATE 76.  ©.  *a*) Lintel 53.  *b*) Lintel 15.  Yaxchilan, Mexico.

*a*

*b*

PLATE 77.   ©.   *a*) Lintel 1.   *b*) Lintel 3.   Piedras Negras, Guatemala.

PLATE 78. ©. *a*) Fragment of stone relief, Piedras Negras, Guatemala. *b*) Fragment of stone relief, Jonuta, Mexico.

PLATE 79. ©.  Figures in stucco relief, Palace Group, Palenque, Mexico.

*b*

*a*

PLATE 80. ©. *a*, *b*, and *c*) Figures in stucco relief from tomb walls, Comalcalco, Mexico. *d*) Model of reconstructed tomb.

a

b

PLATE 81.   ©.   a) Stone tablet from Palenque, Mexico.   b) Maya astronomer seated
on a hieroglyph, Chiapas, Mexico.

*a*

*b*

*c*

PLATE 82. ©. Round stone reliefs: *a*) Ball-court marker, Copan, Honduras; *b*) small altar, Tonina, Mexico; *c*) Ball-court marker, Chinkultic, Mexico.

*a*

*b*

*c*

PLATE 83.   ©.   Sculptured profiles:   *a*) Piedras Negras, Guatemala;   *b*) Copan, Honduras;
*c*) El Tajin, Papantla, Mexico.

PLATE 84.  ©.  *a*) Detail of Maya lintel, El Chicozapote, Mexico.  *b*) Zapotec sculptured stone, Zachilla, Mexico.

PLATE 85.  ©.  *a*) Head of a monster.  *b*) Maya head.  Copan, Honduras.

PLATE 86.  ©.  Stucco heads:  *a*) Palenque, Mexico;  *b*) Piedras Negras, Guatemala;  *c*) Uxmal, Mexico;
*d*) Louisville, British Honduras.

PLATE 87.   ©.   Human figure of stone from the Hieroglyphic Stairway, Copan, Honduras.

*a*

*b*

*c*

*d*

PLATE 88. Ⓒ. Stone heads: *a*) Copan, Honduras; *b*) Quiriguá, Guatemala; *c*) provenience unknown; *d*) Copan.

*a*

*b*

PLATE 89. ⓒ. Two Maize-god-type sculptures, Copan, Honduras.

PLATE 90.　©.　Bust of the Maize-god, Copan, Honduras.

PLATE 91. ©. Plastic decorations on the bases of buildings, Mexico: *a*) Palenque; *b*) Monte Alban; *c*) Acanceh; *d*) Chichen Itzá.

*b*

*a*

PLATE 92.  ©.  *a*) Detail of mural, showing warrior seated on jaguar throne, Temple of Chacmool, Chichen Itzá, Mexico.
*b*) Jaguar throne from inner temple, El Castillo, Chichen Itzá.

*a*

*b*

PLATE 93. ©. *a*) Atlantean columns, Chichen Itzá, Mexico. *b*) Chacmool from Chichen Itzá.

*a*

*b*

*c*

*d*

PLATE 94. ©. Sculptured marble vases, Ulua Valley, Honduras.

*a*

*b*

PLATE 95.   ©.   Sculptured marble vases, Ulua Valley, Honduras.

PLATE 96. ©. Seated stone figures: *a*) Chichicastenango, Guatemala; *b*) Rio Frio, Costa Rica.

*a*                                                              *b*

*c*                                            *d*

PLATE 97.   ©.   *a* and *b*) Sculptured "axes," Guatemala.   *c* and *d*) Stone figures, Costa Rica.

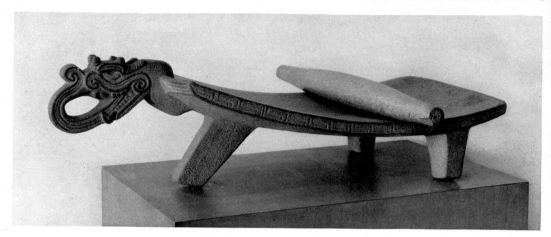

*a*

*b*

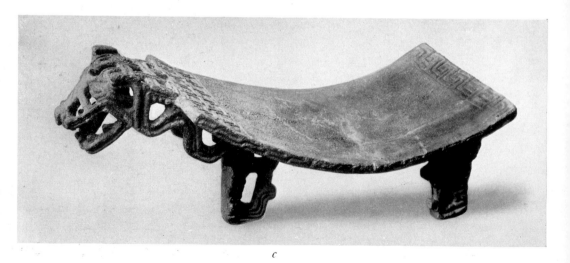

*c*

PLATE 98. ©. Sculptured *metates* (grinding stones): *a*) Guatemala; *b*) Costa Rica; *c*) Nicaragua.

*a*

*b*

*c*

PLATE 99.   ©.   *a*) Monolith E, Cerro Sechin, Peru.   *b*) Stela Raimondi,
Chavin de Huántar, Peru.   *c*) Giant statue, Tiahuanaco, Bolivia.

*a*

*b*

PLATE 100.  ©.  Carved stone bowls:  *a*) Chavin;  *b*) Highland Inca.

# POTTERY

*a*

*b*

*c*

*d*

*e*

PLATE 101.  ©.  Pottery shapes from Arizona.

*a*

*b*

*c*

PLATE 102.   ©.   Water jars, or *ollas*:   *a*) Arizona;   *b*) Colorado;   *c*) New Mexico.

*a*

*b*

*c*

*d*

*e*

*f*

PLATE 103. ©. Various painted pottery: *a, b, c,* and *f*) Arizona; *d*) New Mexico; *e*) Colorado.

*a*

*b*

*c*

PLATE 104.   ©.   *a*) Three Pueblo mugs, Navaho Canyon, Arizona.   *b*) Double jar, Mesa Verde, Colorado.   *c*) Pottery dipper, New Mexico.

*a*

*b*

*c*

*d*

PLATE 105.   ⓒ.   Various types of black-and-white and colored ware:   *a*) New Mexico;   *b*) Colorado;
*c*) Arizona;   *d*) northern Mexico.

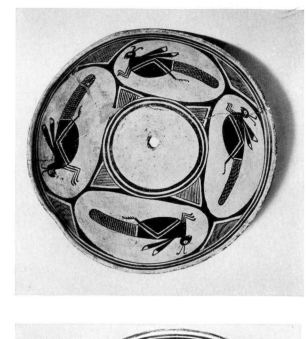

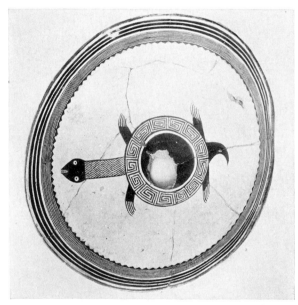

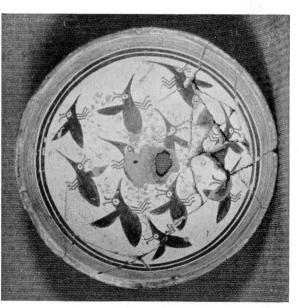

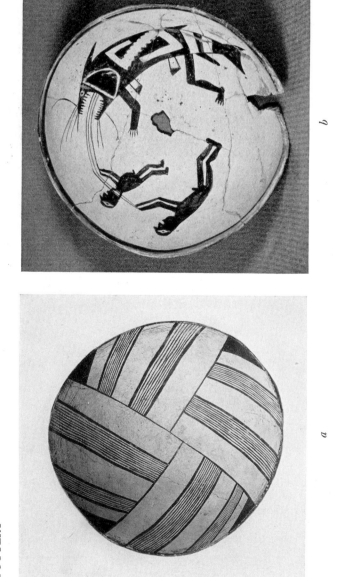

a

b

c

d

e

f

PLATE 106. ⓒ. Mimbres bowls, New Mexico.

a                              b                              c

d                                              e

PLATE 107.  ©.  Mimbres bowls, New Mexico.

*a*

*b*

*c*

*d*

PLATE 108.  ©.  *a* and *b*) Painted water bottles, Arkansas.  *c*) Incised bowl, Louisiana.
*d*) Burial urn with stamped decoration, Georgia.

*a*

*b*

*c*                                         *d*

PLATE 109. ©.  *a*) Precipitation jar, Missouri.  *b*) Black-ware bottles, Arkansas.  *c*) Horned
snake effigy bowl, Arkansas.  *d*) Incised brown-ware bottle, Louisiana.

*a*

*b*

*c*

PLATE 110.   ©.   Early pottery shapes:   *a*) Monte Alban;   *b* and *c*) Teotihuacan.

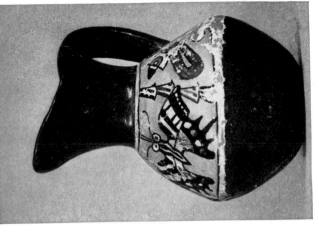

*a*

*b*

*c*

*d*

*e*

*f*

PLATE 111. © . Pitchers: *a*) Toluca Valley ; *b*) Oaxaca ; *c*) Puebla. Tripods: *d*, *e*, and *f*) Oaxaca.

*a*

*b*

*c*

PLATE 112. ©. Tarascan figures in clay.

a

b

c

d                                              e

PLATE 113.  ©.  *a*) Tarascan mother and child.  *b*) Miniature warrior.  *c*) Figure on
couch, northwest Mexico.  *d* and *e*) "Pretty ladies," Valley of Mexico.

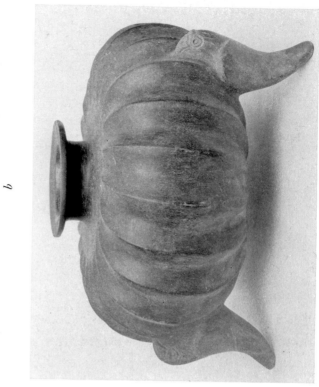

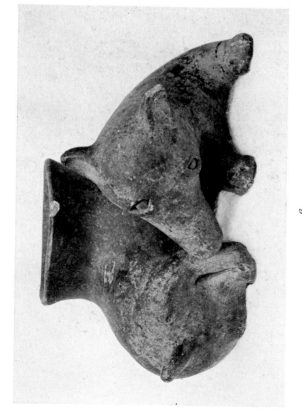

*a*

*b*

*c*

*d*

PLATE 114.  ©.  Pottery types, Colima.

*a*

*b*

*c*

*d*

PLATE 115.  ©.  *a* and *b*) Tarascan warriors.  *c*) Small standing figure, Chiapas.
*d*) Seated figure, central Vera Cruz.

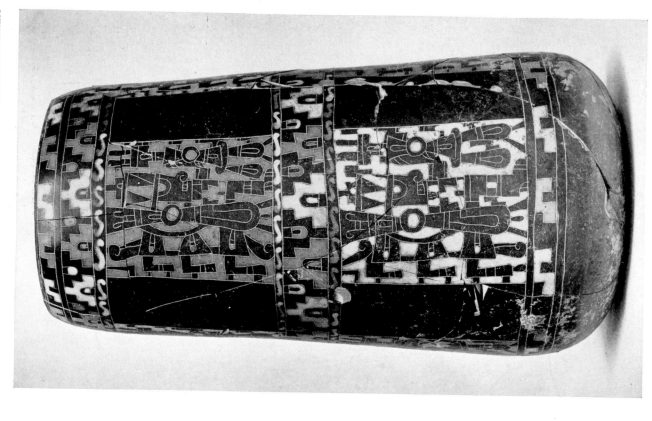

*a*

*b*

*c*

*d*

PLATE 116. ©. *a* and *b*) Cholula plates. *c*) Mixtec serpent effigy jar. *d*) Cylindrical vase, Huaxtec?.

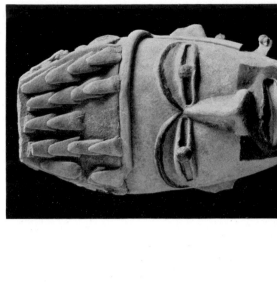

*c*

*e*

*b*

*a*

*d*

PLATE 117. ⓒ. Clay heads from different cultures:
*a*) Zacatenco. D. F.; *b*) Vera Cruz?; *c*) Guadalajara,
Jalisco; *d*) Vera Cruz; *e*) Vera Cruz?.

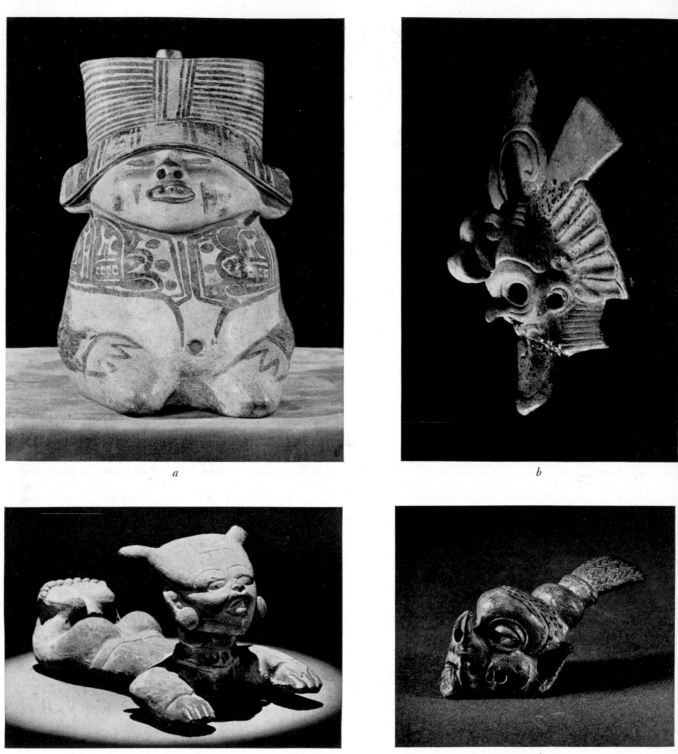

PLATE 118. ©. *a*) Figurine, Tempoal. *b*) Masquette of moan bird. *c*) Pottery whistle. *d*) Bat head. Vera Cruz.

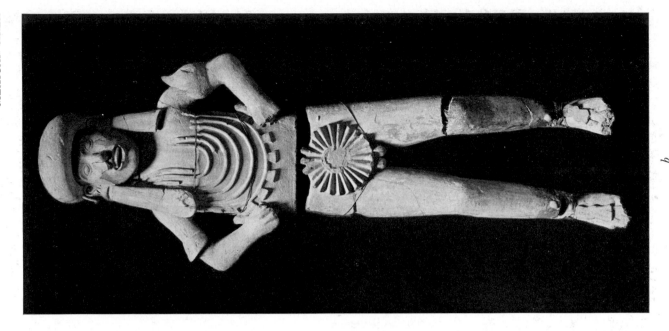

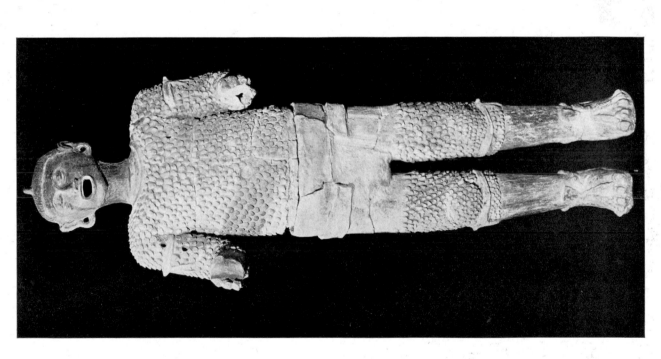

PLATE 119.  ©.  Large Aztec terra-cotta figures.

b

a

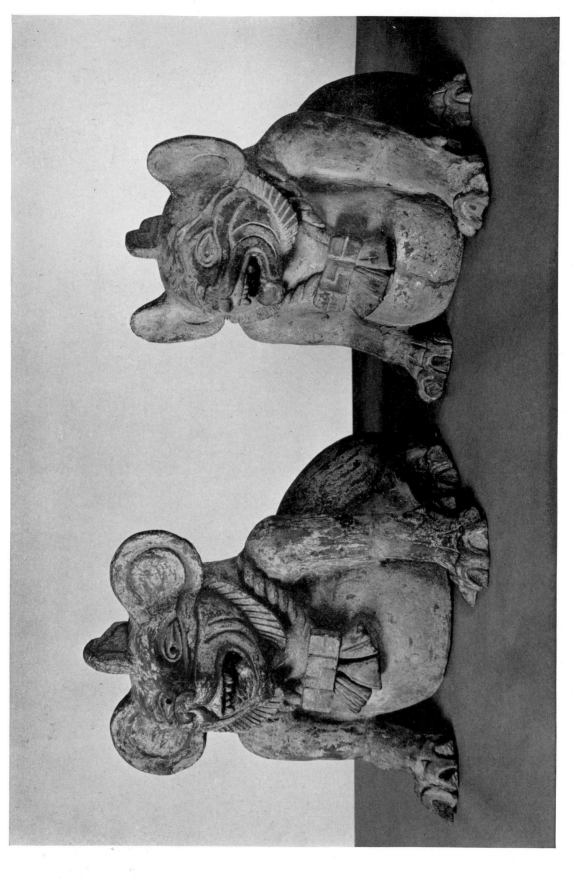

PLATE 120.  ©.  Zapotec Messenger Dogs of the Gods, Oaxaca.

*c*

*b*

*a*

PLATE 121. ©. Effigy funerary urns and incense burner, Oaxaca.

*a*

*b*

*c*

*d*

PLATE 122.   ©.   Zapotec incense burners, Oaxaca.

*a*                                         *b*

*c*                                         *d*

PLATE 123.   ©.   Representations of human figures, Oaxaca.

*a*

*b*

*c*

PLATE 124.  ©.  *a*) Standing figure.  *b*) Vessel with carved medallion.  *c*) Large seated statue.  Oaxaca.

*a*

*b*

*c*

PLATE 125.  ©.  *a*) Incense burner, Puebla, Mexico.  *b*) Incense burner, Guatemala.  *c*) Large
vessel, Guatemala.

*a*

*b*

*c*

PLATE 126.   ©.   *a*) Undecorated vessels, British Honduras.   *b*) Polychrome funerary jar, Chiapas, Mexico.
*c*) Painted beaker, Vera Cruz, Mexico.

*a*

*b*

*c*

*d*

PLATE 127. Ⓒ. *a* and *b*) Effigy vases, Kaminaljuyú, Guatemala. *c*) Brownish tripod vessel with lid, Kaminaljuyú. *d*) Black-ware effigy, Uaxactun.

*By special permission of Carnegie Institution of Washington.*

*a*

*b*

*c*

PLATE 128. ©. *a* and *c*) Stuccoed tripod vessel with calligraphic decoration, Uaxactun, Guatemala, and unrolled design. *By special permission of Carnegie Institution of Washington.* *b*) Stuccoed tripod vase with painted decoration, Kaminaljuyú.

*a*

*b*

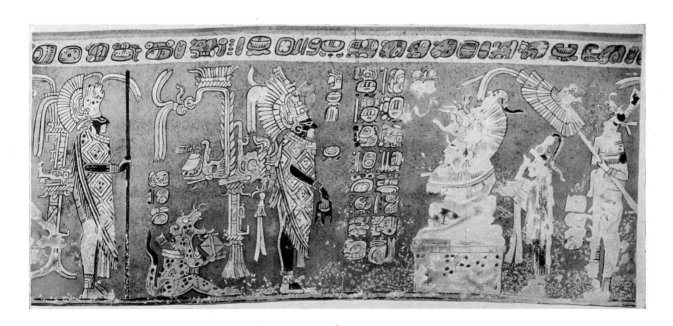

*c*

PLATE 129.  ©.  *a* and *c*) Cylindrical vase with painted decoration, Uaxactun, Guatemala,
and unrolled design.  *b*) Interior design of painted tripod bowl, Holmul.

*a*

*b*

*c*

*d*

PLATE 130. ©. *a* and *c*) Painted vase with warriors, Chamá, Guatemala, and
unrolled design. *b* and *d*) Painted vase with dignitary borne on a journey, Ratinlixul,
and unrolled design.

*a*

*b*

*c*

*d*

PLATE 131.   ©.   Polychrome vases of different shapes:   *a*) Nebaj district, Guatemala;   *b*) Chamá,
Guatemala;   *c*) Copan, Honduras;   *d*) El Salvador?.

PLATE 132. ©. Vases representing human heads, Guatemala: *a*) Quiriguá; *b*) Kaminaljuyú.

*a*

*b*

*c*

*d*

PLATE 133.  ©.  Figurines from Mexico:  *a* and *c*) Yucatan?;  *b*) Palenque;  *d*) Tabasco.

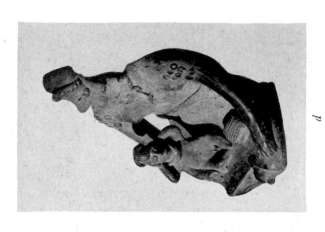

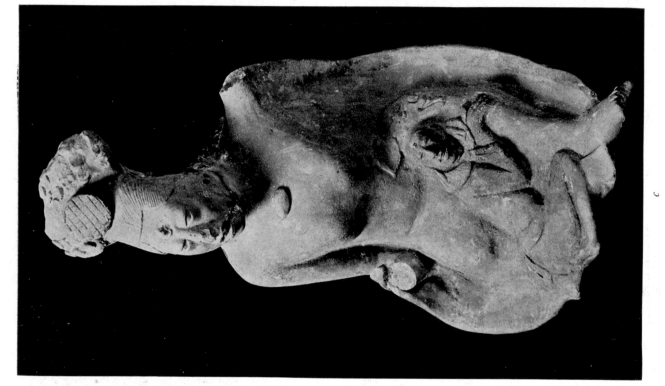

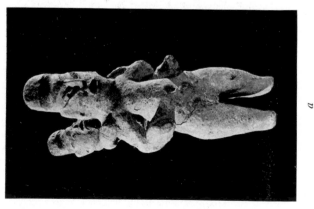

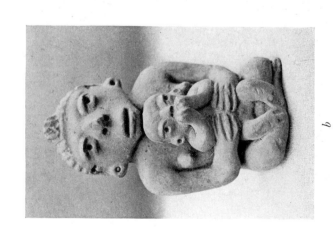

PLATE 134. ©. Variations on a theme: *a*) Cuernavaca, Mexico; *b*) Solcajá, Guatemala; *c*) Campeche, Mexico; *d*) Tarascan region, Mexico; *e*) near Palenque, Mexico.

*a*

*b*

*c*

PLATE 135.  ©.  Vases with incised figural decoration:  *a*) Yucatan?, Mexico;  *b*) Zacualpa, Guatemala;
*c*) Asunción Mita, Guatemala.

*a*

*b*

*c*

PLATE 136. ⓒ. Relief vases from Guatemala: *a*) Uaxactun; *b*) Zacualpa; *c*) Kaminaljuyú.
*By special permission of Carnegie Institution of Washington.*

*a*

*b*

PLATE 137.  ©.  Relief vases from Mexico:  *a*) Yucatan?;  *b*) Peto, Yucatan.

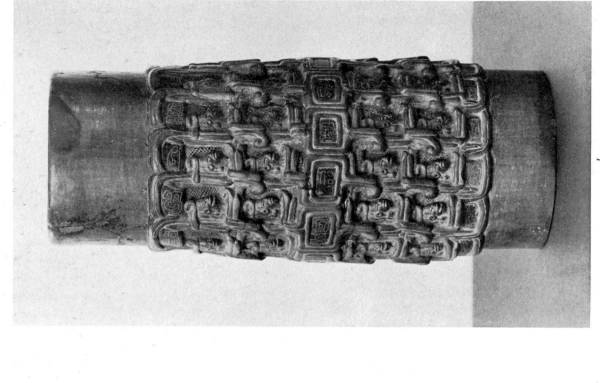

*b*

*a*

PLATE 138.  ©.  *a*) Sculptured bowl, San Augustín Acasaguastlán, Guatemala.  *b*) Tall relief vase, Ataco, El Salvador.

*a*

*b*

*c*                                          *d*

PLATE 139.  Ⓒ.  *a*) Beaker with relief decoration, Guatemala?.  *b*) Beaker with relief, incision, and painted decoration, Jutiapa, Guatemala.  *c*) Buff beaker with glyphs in relief, Tonacatepeque, El Salvador. *d*) Jar with incised glyphs and painted decoration, Ulua Valley, Honduras.

PLATE 140. ©. Small flasks: *a*) Honduras; *b, c,* and *d*) El Salvador; *e*) Yucatan, Mexico; *f, g,* and *h*) El Salvador.

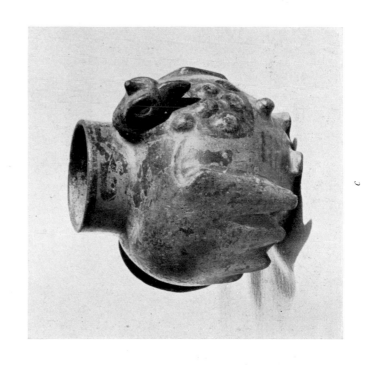

PLATE 141. ©. Various shapes from the Guatemalan highlands: *a*) Kaminaljuyú; *b*) Sololá?; *c*) Soyaba; *d*) Nebaj.

*a*                                     *b*                                     *c*

*d*                                                                    *e*

PLATE 142. ©. *a* and *b*) Cylindrical jars with painted decoration, El Salvador. *c*) Vessel with
painted decoration, Coclé, Panama. *d* and *e*) Mayoid painted vases, El Salvador and
Ulua Valley, Honduras.

c

b

a

PLATE 143.  ⓒ.  Cylindrical vessels with animal handles, Honduras.

*a*

*b*

*c*

PLATE 144.   ©.   Incense burner lids:   *a*) Guatemala;   *b*) Nicaragua;   *c*) Costa Rica.

*a*

*b*

*c*

*d*

PLATE 145. ©. *a*) Animal effigy pot with negative painting, Nicoya, Costa Rica. *b*) Negative painted jar with rattle base, Costa Rica. *c*) Polychrome tripod bowl, Nicaragua. *d*) Animal effigy jar with polychrome decoration, Zacualpa, Guatemala.

*c*

*e*

*b*

*d*

*a*

PLATE 146. ©. Ceramic shapes, Coclé, Panama.

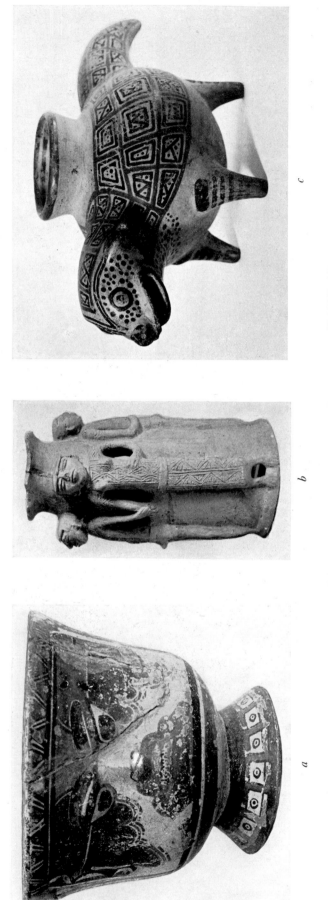

*c*

*f*

*b*

*e*

*a*

*d*

PLATE 148. ©. Various pottery shapes from various cultures: *a*) Nicaragua; *b*) Colombia; *c*) Panama; *d*) Costa Rica; *e*) Venezuela; *f*) Panama.

*a*

*b*

*c*

*d*

PLATE 149.  ©.  *a*) Tripod bowl with monkey figures, Panama.   *b*) Clay stool, Panama.   *c*) Tripod
with monkeys, Costa Rica.   *d*) Bottle with animal decoration, Brazil.

PLATE 150.  ©.   *a* and *b*) Vessels with human figures, Colombia.   *c* and *d*) Alligator-ware jars, Brazil.

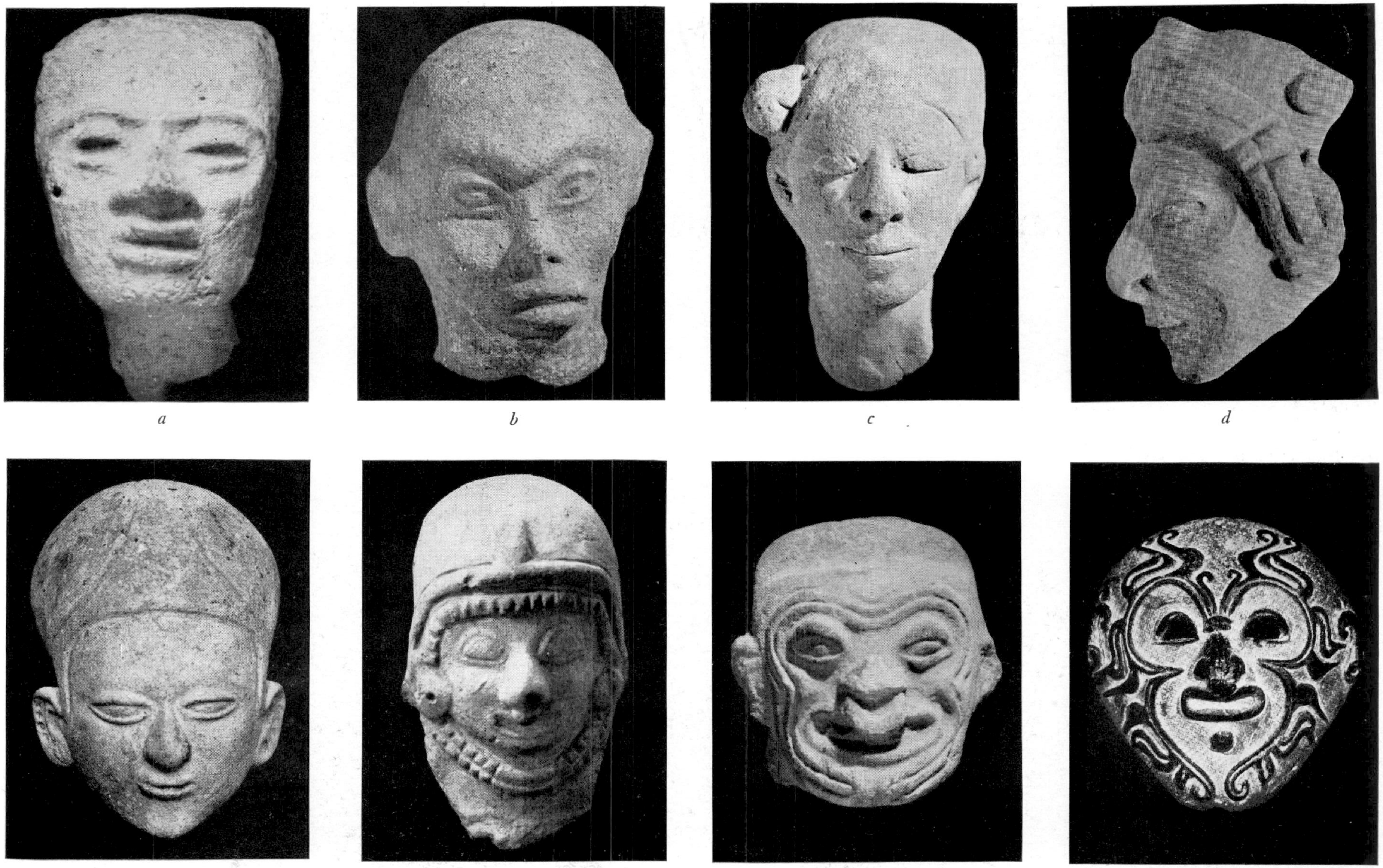

*a* *b* *c* *d*

*e* *f* *g* *h*

PLATE 151. ©. Small pottery heads: *a*) Venezuela; *b-h*) Ecuador.

*b*

*a*

PLATE 152.  ©.  Mochica stirrup-spout vessels:  *a*) The Trumpeter;  *b*) warrior on a raft.  Peru.

*a*

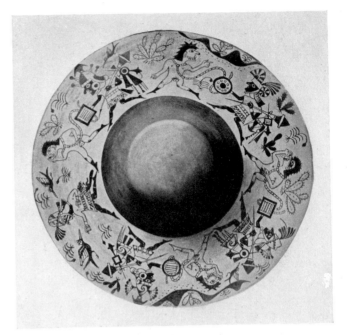

*b*

*c*

*d*

PLATE 153. ⓒ. Mochica vessels with story-telling decoration.

*a*

*b*

*c*

*d*

PLATE 154. ©. Mochica effigy vessels showing striking poses.

*a*

*b*

*c*

*d*

PLATE 155. Ⓒ. Scenes of Mochica and Chimu life.

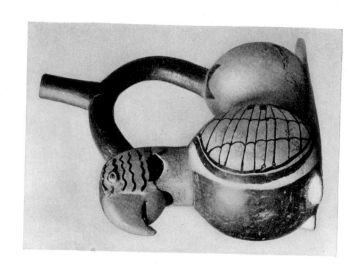

c

e

b

a

d

PLATE 156. ©. Mochica and Chimu water jars with animal subjects.

*a*

*b*

*c*

*d*

PLATE 157.  ©.  Animal representations, Peru and Ecuador.

*a*

*b*

*c*

*d*

PLATE 158.  ©.  *a*) Mochica Potato Mother.  *b*) Chimu double jar with pressed relief.  *c* and *d*) Chimu shapes of a vegetable and fruit.

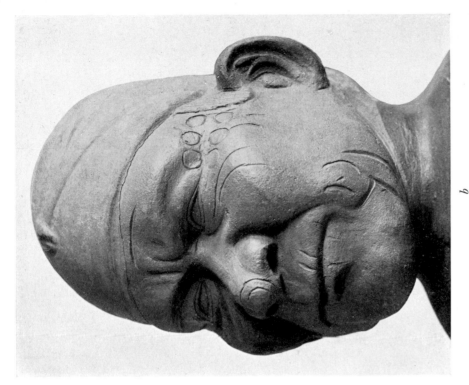

*b*

*a*

PLATE 159. ©. Mochica portrait vessels.

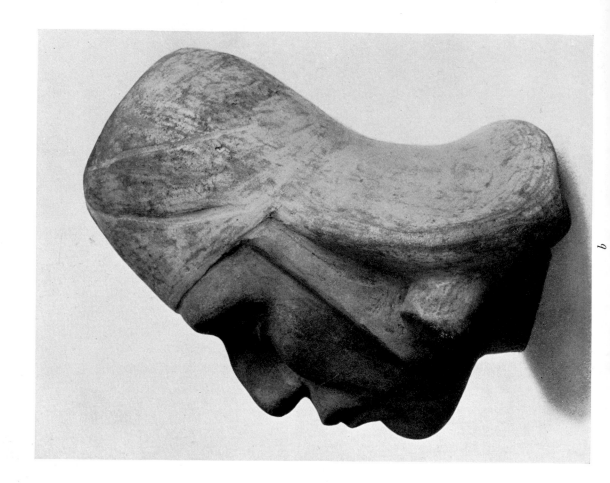

*a*

*b*

PLATE 160. ⓒ. Mochica portrait vessels.

POTTERY

*c*

*b*

*a*

*d*

PLATE 161. ©. *a*) Mochica effigy jar. *b* and *c*) Nazca effigy jars. *d*) Mochica effigies, depicting ravages of disease.

*c*

*f*

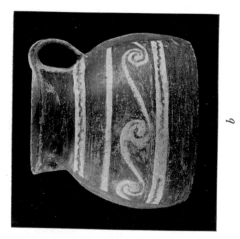

*b*

*e*

*a*

*d*

PLATE 162. ⓒ. Various shapes from South Coast of Peru and Chile.

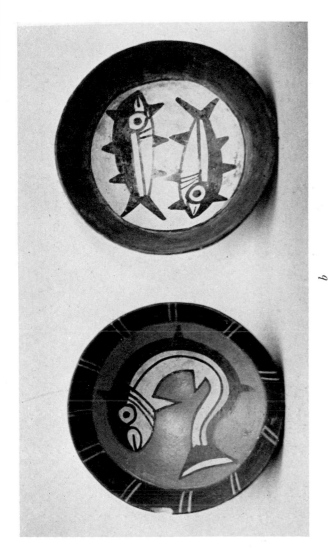

*b*

*d*

*a*

*c*

PLATE 163. ⓒ. Painted ware: *a* and
*c*) Coast Tiahuanaco; *b* and *d*) Nazca.

*a*

*b*

*c*

*d*

PLATE 164.  ©.  *a*) Painted jar with handles, Coast Tiahuanaco.  *b, c,* and *d*) Painted jars, Nazca.

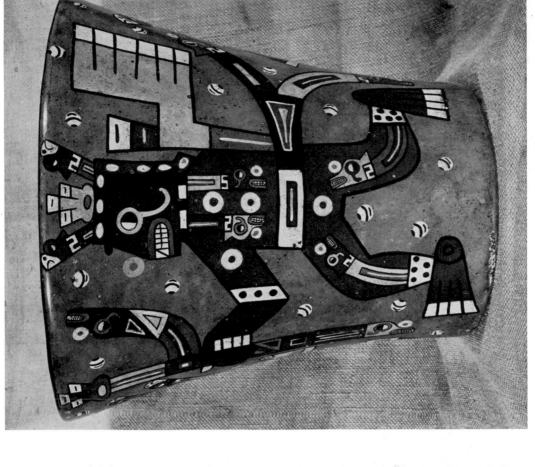

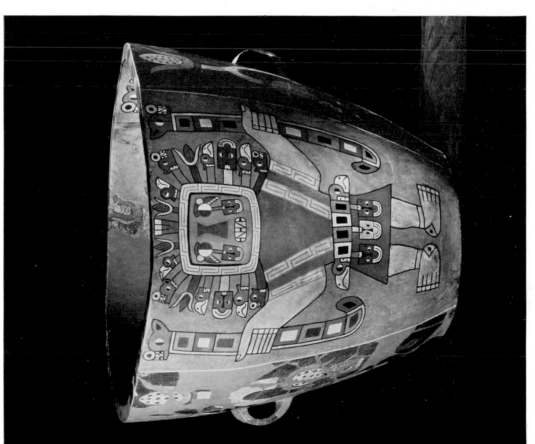

*a*

*b*

PLATE 165. ©. Large ceremonial urns in Coast Tiahuanaco style: *a*) Nazca region; *b*) South Coast of Peru.

*a*

*b*

PLATE 166. ©. Bowls and jars in Classic and Decadent Tiahuanaco style, Tiahuanaco, Bolivia.

*a*

*b*

*c*

*d*

PLATE 167. © Modulations of a basic shape: *a*) Decadent Tiahuanaco; *b*) Late Coast Tiahuanaco; *c* and *d*) Ica.

PLATE 168. © Inca aryballos.

# WEAVING

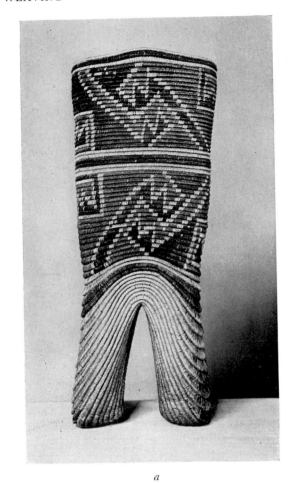

*b*

*a*

*c*

*d*

PLATE 169. ©. *a*) Cliff-dweller basketry "cradle," Utah, Pueblo III. *b*) Burden basket, Arizona, Basket Maker III. *c*) Baskets from Arizona: two larger, Basket Maker III; smaller, Pueblo I. *d*) Twined sandals, Arizona, Basket Maker III.

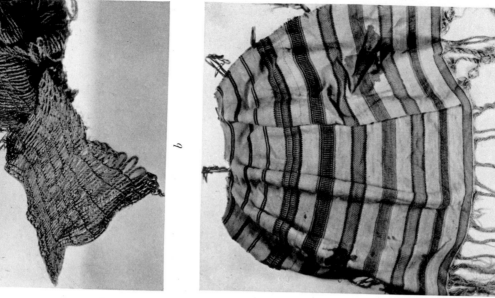

PLATE 170. ©. *a*) Pueblo child's desiccated body wrapped in feather and deerskin blankets, New Mexico. *b*) Yucca fiber foundation for rabbit-skin blanket, Arizona, Basket Maker or Pueblo. *c*) Basket Maker burden strap of yucca, Colorado. *d*) Twined woven fabric, Basket Maker III.

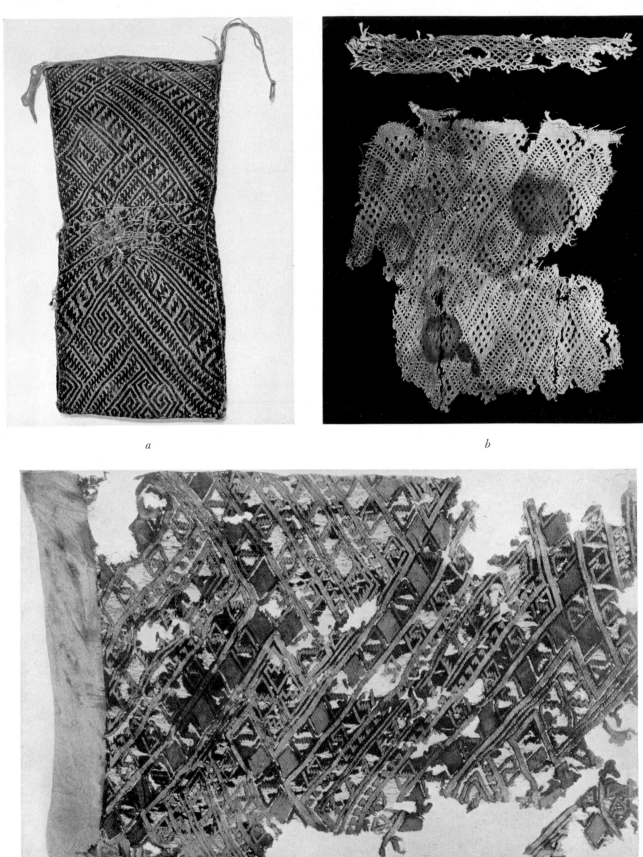

*a*

*b*

*c*

PLATE 171.  ©.  *a*) Pueblo cotton bag woven in damask technique, Arizona.  *b*) Lacy openwork
in cotton, New Mexico, Pueblo III.  *c*) Fragment of cotton kilt, Utah, Pueblo IV.

*a*

*b*

PLATE 172.   ©.   *a*) Navaho women carding, spinning, and weaving wool, Arizona.   *b*) Modern
Pueblo embroidered shirt, New Mexico.

*a*

*c*

*b*

PLATE 173. ©. *a*) Indian weaver, Guatemalan highlands. *b*) Aztec blankets as represented
in the Tribute Roll of Montezuma. *c*) Girl's modern blouse, Guatemala.

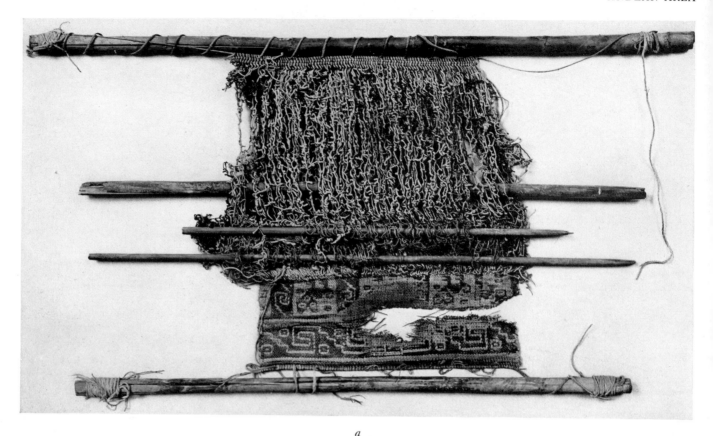

*a*

*b*

*c*

PLATE 174. ©. *a*) Girdle-back loom with partly woven double cloth, Ica?. *b*) Spindles and bobbins, Ica?.
*c*) Double cloth, Ica.

*a*

*b*

*c*

PLATE 175. ⓒ.  *a*) Section of fringed shawl with over-all embroidery, Paracas.  *b*) Wool embroidery and brocade on cotton, Nazca.  *c*) Interlocking warp (left) and patchwork tie-dye (right), Coast Tiahuanaco?.

*a*

*b*

*c*

PLATE 176.  ©.  Embroidery:  *a*) Coast Tiahuanaco;  *b*) Paracas;  *c*) Nazca.

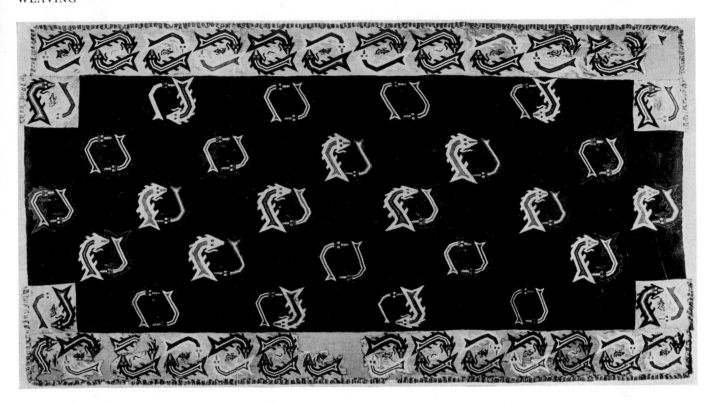

*a*

*b*

PLATE 177.  ©.   Paracas embroidery.

*c*

*a*

*b*

PLATE 178.  ©.  Coast Tiahuanaco tapestry:  *a*) poncho, or shirt;  *b*) detail of a band;  *c*) section of garment.

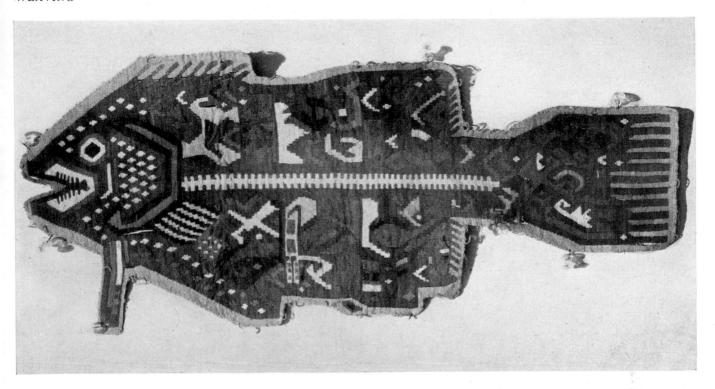

*a*

*b*

*c*

PLATE 179.  ©.  Tapestry:  *a*) Chimu?;  *b*) Ica;  *c*) Coast Tiahuanaco.

*a*

*b*

*c*

PLATE 180. Ⓒ. Bags, or pouches: *a*) Inca?; *b*) Late Coast Tiahuanaco; *c*) Coast Tiahuanaco.

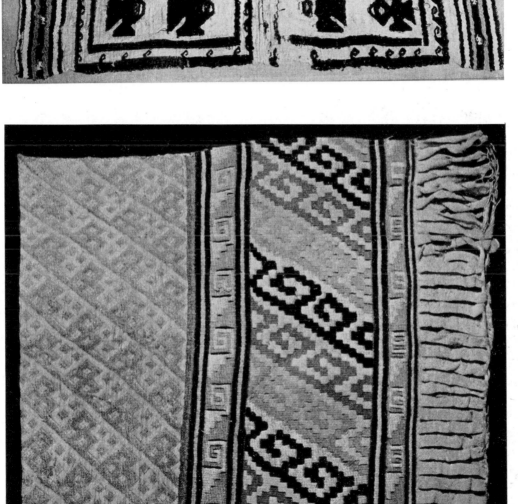

PLATE 181. ©. *a*) Brocade with tapestry border, Ica? *b*) Ica brocade, Nazca Valley.

*a*                                              *b*

*c*

PLATE 182.  ©.  Painted plain-woven cloth:  *a*) Chimu?;  *b*) Coast Tiahuanaco?;  *c*) Late Coast Tiahuanaco?.

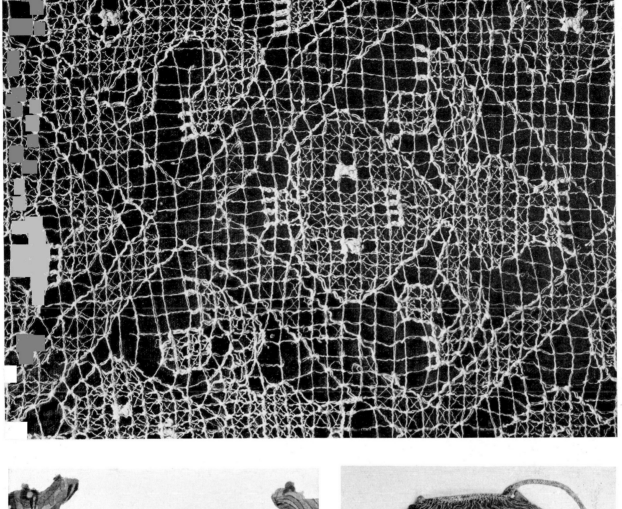

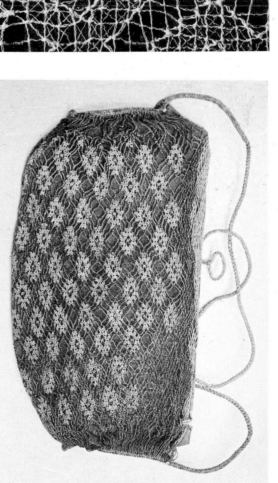

*c*

*a*

*b*

PLATE 183. ©. *a*) Painted cloth, Nazca. *b*) Hairnet of maguey fiber, Chimu?. *c*) Embroidered lacelike gauze, Chimu?.

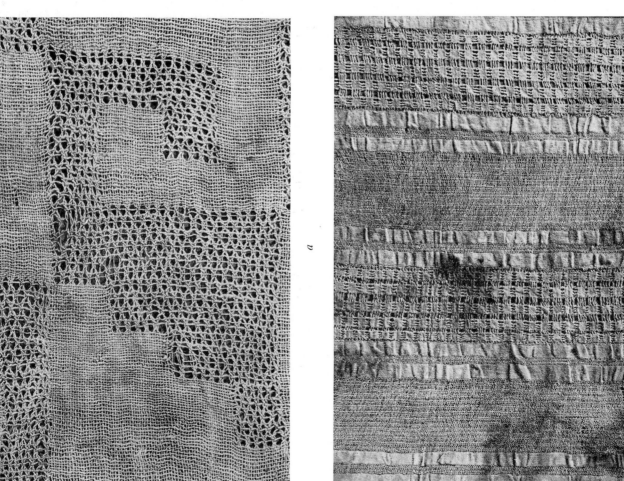

PLATE 184. ©. *a*) Gauze, Nazca.   *b*) Gauze with open weave, Chimu?.   *c*) Openwork with tapestry border, Ica?.

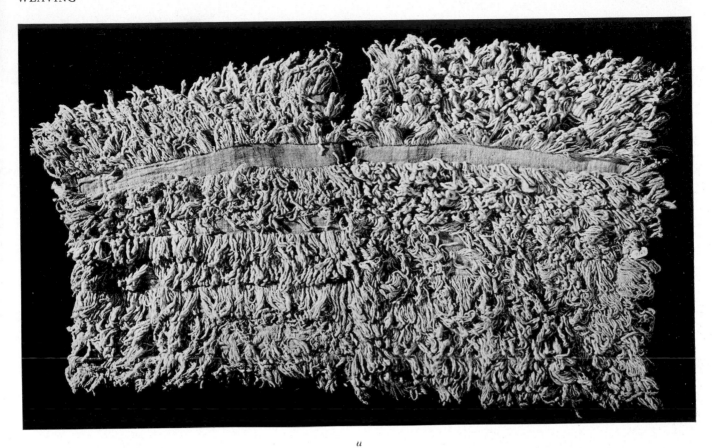

*a*

*b*

*c*

PLATE 185.  ©.  *a*) Poncho in weft-loop weave.  *b*) Openwork tapestry with tassels.  *c*) Tapestry
with tasseled rosettes.   Chimu?.

*a*

*b*

PLATE 186. ©. Plush hats, Coast Tiahuanaco.

PLATE 187.  ©.  Section of Paracas embroidered shawl.

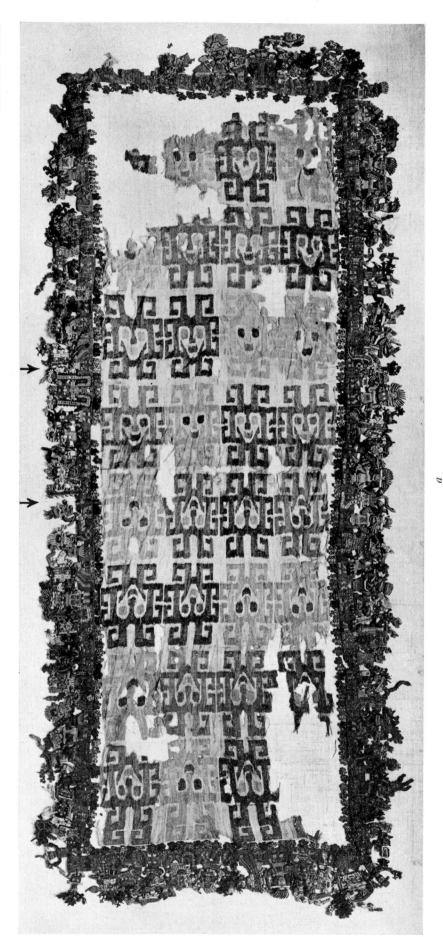

PLATE 188. ©. *a*) Paracas mantle with border in three-dimensional knitting. *b*) Detail of border.

*a*

*b*

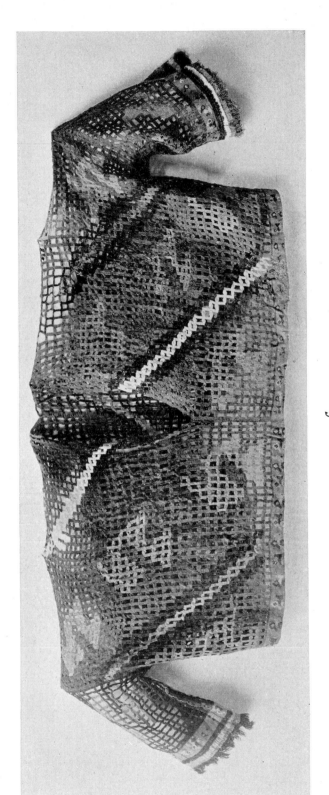

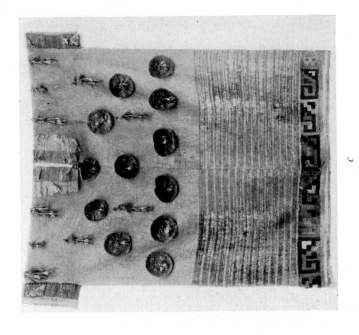

*c*

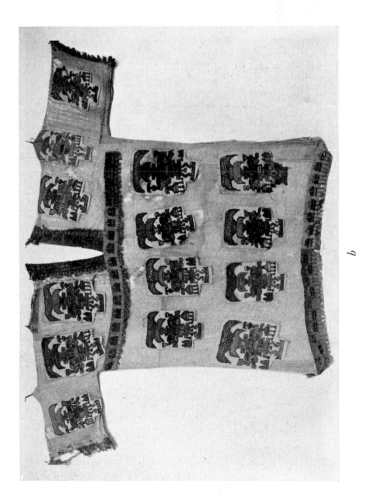

*b*

*a*

PLATE 189. ©. Ponchos: *a*) spaced-warp tapestry, Ica?; *b*) with tapestry medallions, Chimu?; *c*) plain and open weave, with tassels and medallions, Chimu?.

*a*

*b*

PLATE 190.  ©.  Ponchos:  *a*) Late Coast Tiahuanaco?;  *b*) Paracas.

*a*

*b*

*c*                                                                    *d*

PLATE 191.   ©.   Inca tapestry ponchos.

*a*

*b*

PLATE 192. Ⓒ. *a*) Spanish colonial tapestry, Peru, 17th-18th century. *b*) Post-Columbian tapestry poncho, Lake Titicaca, Bolivia, late 16th century.

# METAL-WORK

*a*

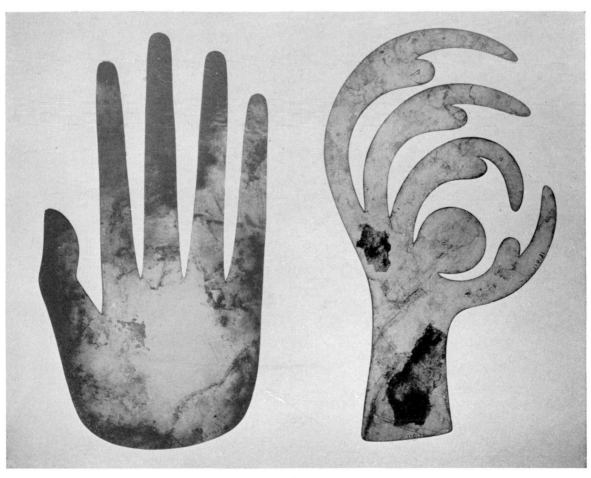

*b*

PLATE 193.  Ⓒ.  *a*) Copper ornaments for clothing.  *b*) Human hand and eagle foot
of mica.  Ohio.

*a*

*b*

*c*

*d*

PLATE 194.  Ⓒ.  *a*) Copper headdress ornament, Tennessee.  *b, c,* and *d*) Human heads
embossed on sheet copper, Oklahoma.

*a*

*b*

*c*

*d*

PLATE 195.   ©.   Variations of a Chavin motif in gold, Lambayeque, Peru.

*a*

*b*

*c*

PLATE 196.  Ⓒ.  Variations of a Chavin motif in silver and wood:  *a*) Coast Tiahuanaco;
*b*) Mochica;  *c*) Late Coast Tiahuanaco.

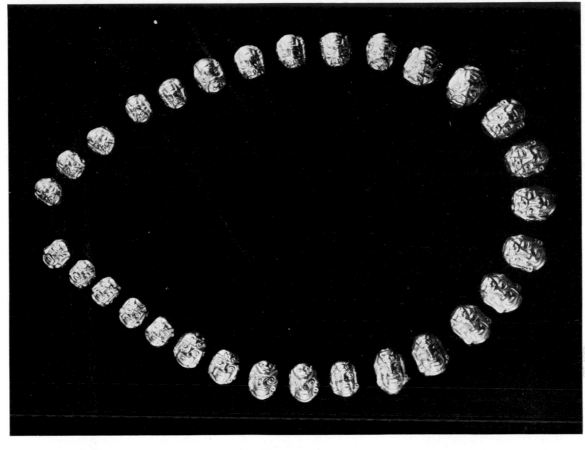

*b*

*a*

PLATE 197. ©. *a*) Chavin gold ear ornaments, Lambayeque. *b*) Mochica gold necklace embossed with human heads.

*c*

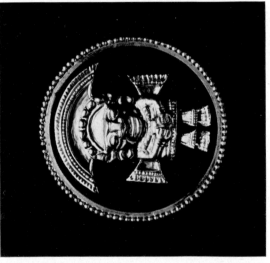

*b*

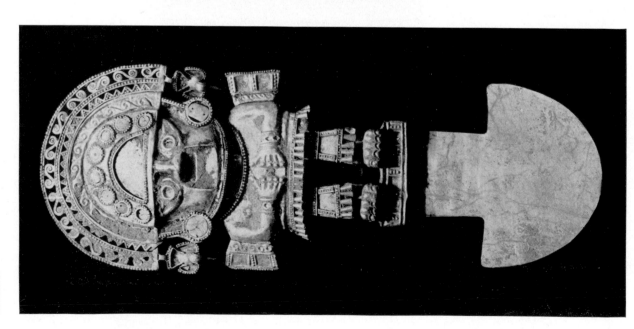

*a*

PLATE 198. ©. *a* and *c*) Chimu gold ceremonial knife with turquoise inlay, Illimo, Lambayeque Valley. *b*) Face of Chimu gold earplug showing same figure, Jayanca.

PLATE 199. ©. Chimu gold objects decorated with human figures: *a*) cup; *b*) plaque; *c*) face of earplug.

*a*                                                      *b*

*c*

PLATE 200.   Ⓒ.   *a*) Gold cup, Classic Tiahuanaco.   *b*) Silver embossed cup, Late Coast Tiahuanaco.   *c*) Gold cups and cup-shaped ear ornaments, Chimu.

*a*

*b*

*c*

PLATE 201.  ⓒ.  *a*) Chimu gold cups with turquoise incrustation, Illimo.  *b*) Chimu silver
cup, embossed, Piura Valley.  *c*) Chimu gold goblet in the shape of a human head, Peru.

*a*

*b*

*c*

PLATE 202.   ©.   *a*) Gold cuff, Mochica?.   *b*) Cast gold figure, Chimu.   *c*) Silver doll with
hinged arms, Chimu.

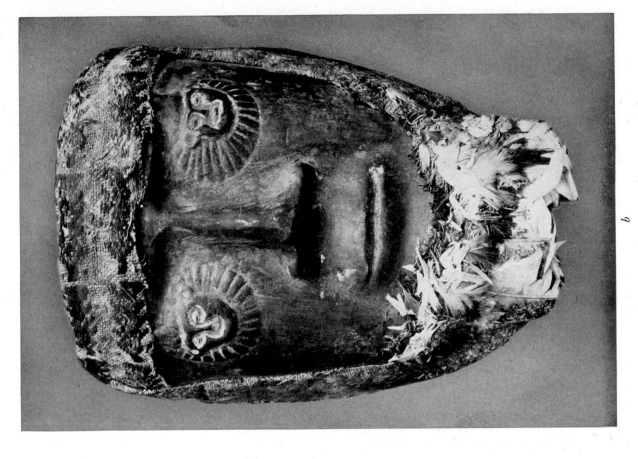

*b*

*a*

PLATE 203. ©. Chimu metal masks from mummy packs: *a*) hammered gold; *b*) base silver with textile and feather additions.

*b*

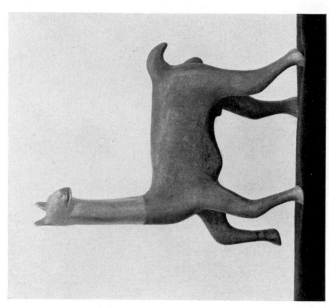

*d*

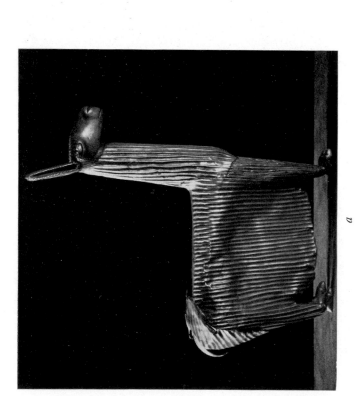

*a*

*c*

PLATE 204. ©. Inca human and animal figurines: *a*) silver alpaca; *b*) man, woman, and llama of cast silver; *c*) copper llama and rider; *d*) alpaca or guanaco, silver alloy with gold head.

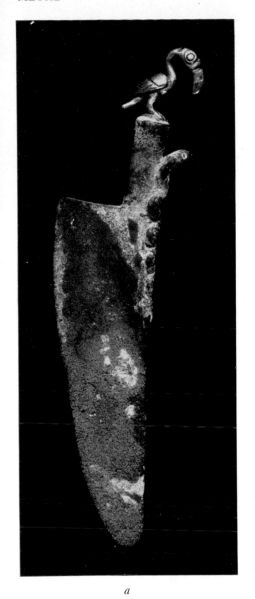

*a*

*b*

*c*

PLATE 205. ©. Inca bronze knives: *a*) with snake and gold pelican; *b*) man and llama; *c*) boy fishing.

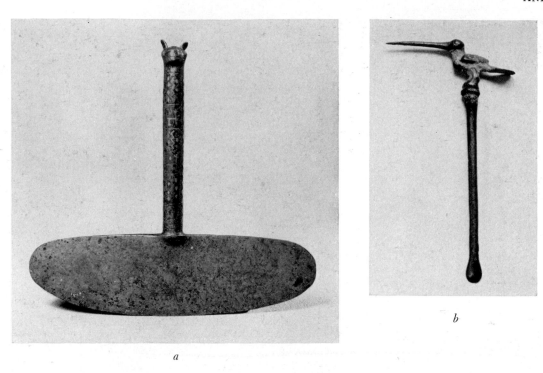

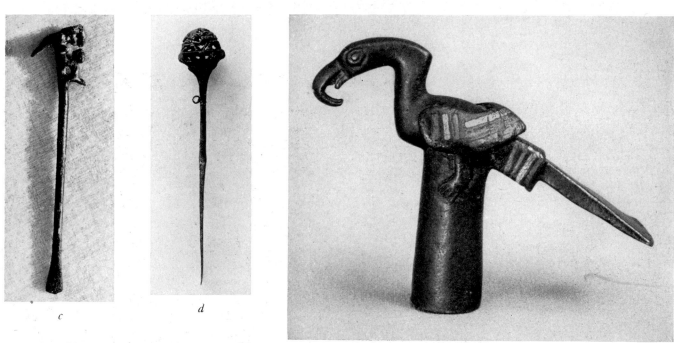

PLATE 206. ©. Inca implements: *a*) bronze knife with inlaid handle shaped into a llama head; *b*) bronze "spoon" with bird; *c*) bronze tool with parrot and monkey; *d*) copper awl or pin with human figures, Inca or Chimu; *e*) bronze adze in the form of a bird, with copper and silver inlay.

*a*

*b*

PLATE 207. ©. *a*) Chavin gold objects for personal use. *b*) Chimu gold plates and stirrup jar.

*a*

*b*

*c*

*d*

PLATE 208.  ©.   *a*) Gold calendar? disk, Peruvian highlands.   *b*) Inca? silver ornaments, Cuzco, Peru. *c* and *d*) Gold disks found near Zacualpa, Guatemala.

*a*

*b*

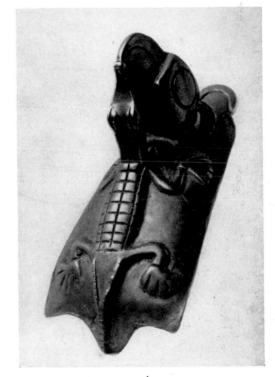

*c*

*d*

PLATE 209.  ©.  Gold animal representations of late cultures:  *a*) beard-tongs with monkeys,
Chimu?;  *b*) earplug with monkeys, Chimu?;  *c*) face of earplug with colibris, Ica;  *d*) pendant
with bird and alligator, Coast Tiahuanaco?.

*a*

*b*

*c*

PLATE 210.  Ⓒ.  *a*) Gold breast ornament.  *b*) Bronze mask.  *c*) Bronze disk.  Ecuador.

*a*

*b*

PLATE 211. Ⓒ. *a*) Gold breastplate. *b*) Small gold mask. Ecuador.

PLATE 212. ©. Gold breastplate, Esmeraldas, Ecuador.

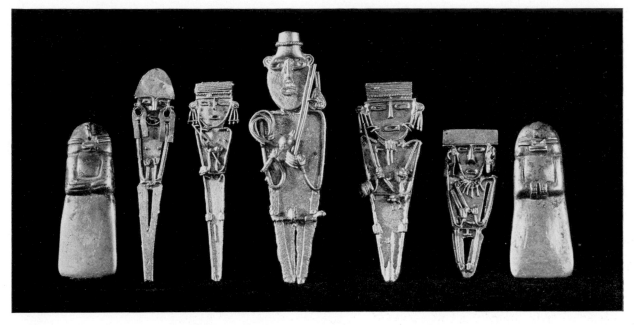

*a*

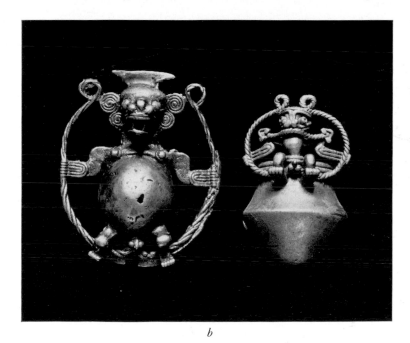

*b*

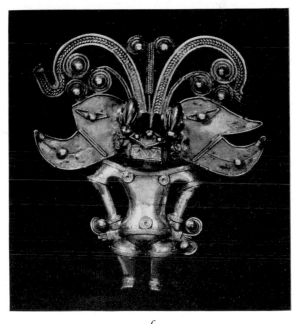

*c*

PLATE 213.  ©.  *a*) Chibcha gold ornaments, Colombia.  *b*) Gold bells, Colombia.  *c*) Gold anthropomorphic figure, Venezuela.

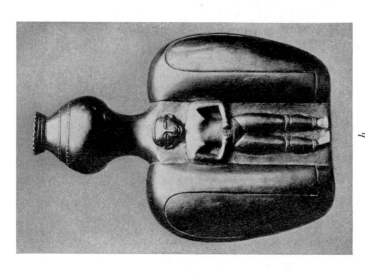

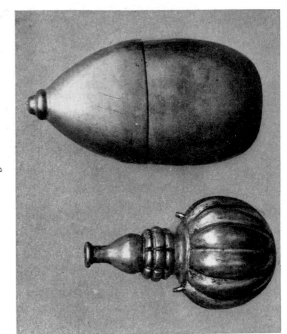

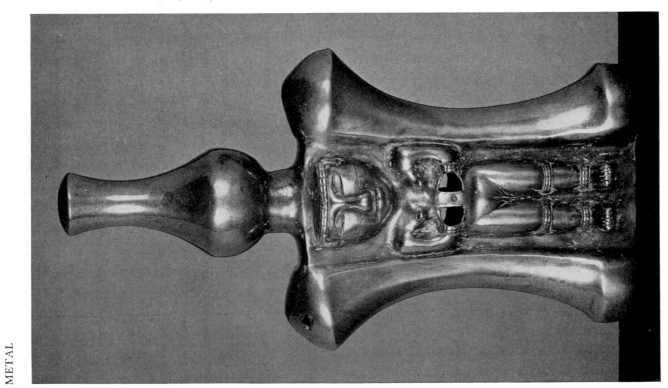

PLATE 214. ©. Quimbaya gold flasks, Antioquia, Colombia.

*a*

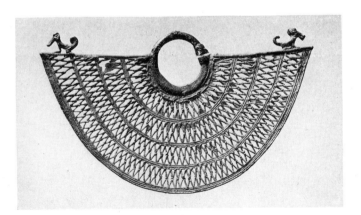

*b*

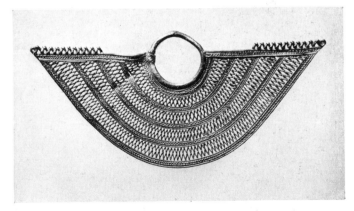

*c*

PLATE 215.   ⓒ.   *a*) Quimbaya gold pendant, blending human and bird elements.   *b* and *c*) Gold nose
ornaments, such as worn by figure above.

*a*

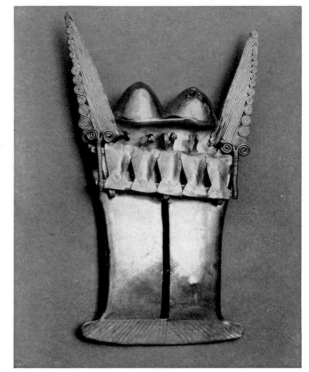

*b*

*c*

PLATE 216.   ©.   Metamorphosis of a Quimbaya figure, Colombia.

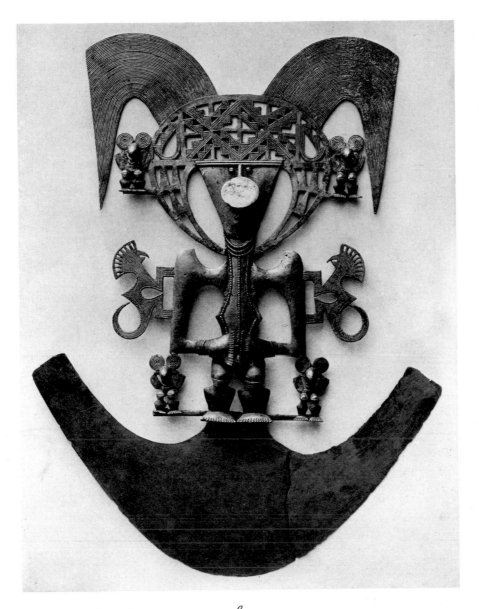

*a*

*b*

PLATE 217. ©. Versions of
knife-shaped pendants, Colombia.

*c*

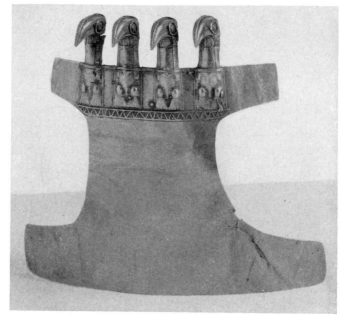

*a*            *b*

*c*            *d*

PLATE 218. ©. Gold plaques, Colombia: *a*) with human figures; *b*) with birds on a tower; *c* and *d*) Quimbaya female idols in cast gold.

METAL

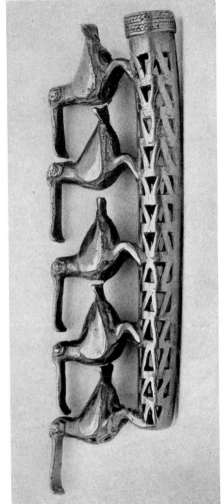

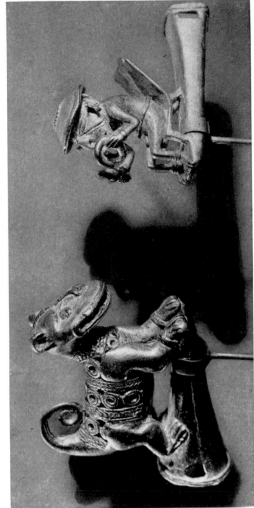

*b*

*c*

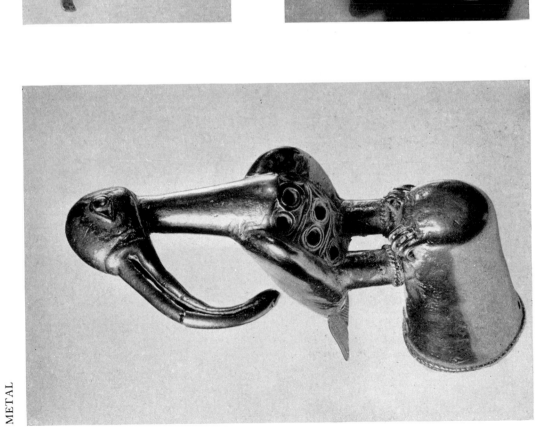

*a*

PLATE 219. ©. Cast gold staff heads, Colombia.

*a*

*b*

PLATE 220.  ©.  Quimbaya gold crown and helmet, Colombia.

*a*

*b*

PLATE 221. ©. Gold helmets, Panama.

PLATE 222. ©. *a*) Gold alligator or crocodile with human prey, Costa Rica. *b*) Gold shark pendant, Chiriqui, Panama. *c* and *d*) Gold alligators carrying conventionalized shapes, Coclé, Panama.

*a*

*b*

PLATE 223.   ©.   Embossed gold plaques, Coclé, Panama.

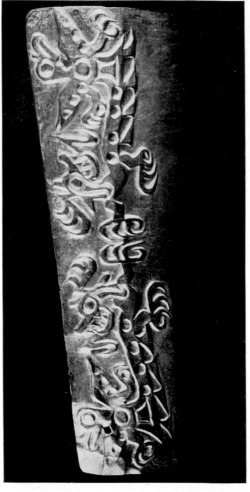

*b*

*d*

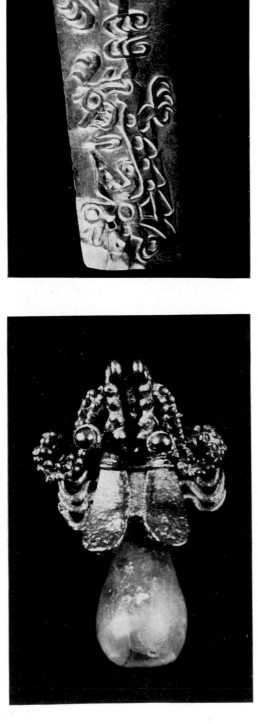

*a*

*c*

PLATE 224. ⓒ. Masterpieces of the jeweler's art, Coclé, Panama: *a*) insect of gold and quartz; *b*) gold cuff with animals in repoussé; *c*) gold dogs or alligator cubs; *d*) gold pendant with inset emerald, in the form of a fantastic animal.

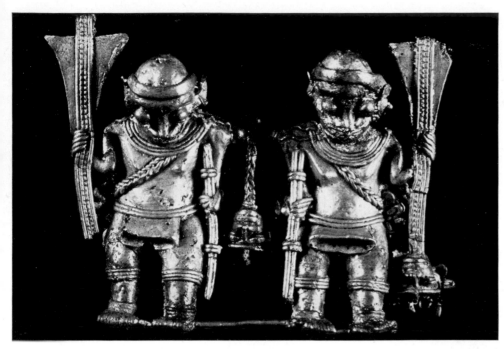

*a*

*b*

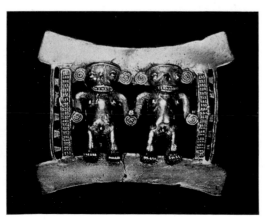

*c*

PLATE 225. ©. Pendants with twin figures: *a*) *tumbaga* alloy, Coclé, Panama; *b*) gold, Chiriqui?, Panama; *c*) gold, Costa Rica.

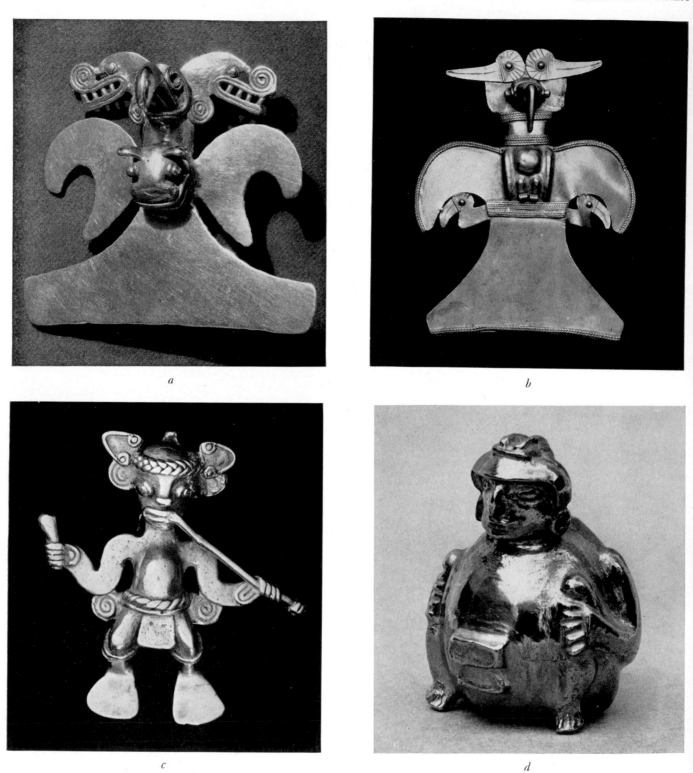

*a*

*b*

*c*

*d*

PLATE 226.  ©.  *a* and *b*) Gold bird pendants, Costa Rica and Colombia.  *c*) Gold figurine, Panama.
*d*) Gold rattle in human shape, Costa Rica.

*a*

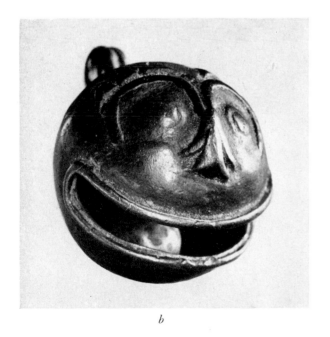

*b*

*c*

PLATE 227.  ©.  *a*) Tarascan copper mask of Xipe-Totec, Mexico.  *b* and *c*) Copper
bells, Honduras and British Honduras.

*a*

*b*

*c*

*d*

*e*

PLATE 228. ©. Finger rings: *a*) gold with eagle pendant, Oaxaca, Mexico; *b*) copper, with human head, El Salvador; *c*) gold, with feathered serpent, Oaxaca; *d*) gold, with glyphs, Oaxaca; *e*) gold with human profile, Oaxaca.

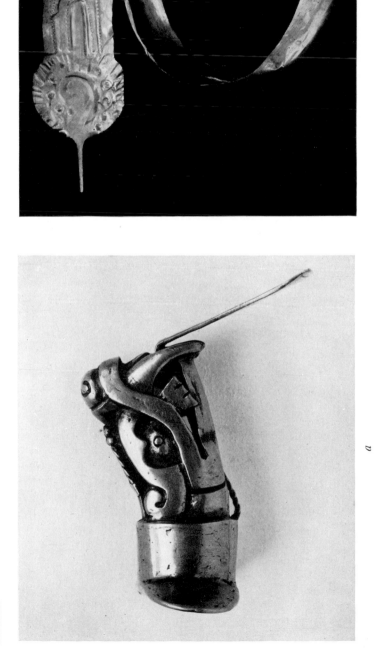

*a*

*b*

*c*

*d*

PLATE 229. ©. Gold articles of personal adornment, Oaxaca: *a* and *c*) lipplugs; *b*) diadem with feather; *d*) bracelet.

*a*

*b*                                                           *c*

PLATE 230.  ©.  Necklaces:  *a* and *c*) gold, Tomb 7, Monte Alban, Oaxaca;  *b*) silver and copper alloy,
Texcoco, Mexico.

*a*

*b*

*c*

PLATE 231.   ©.   *a*) Cast gold pectoral of Jaguar-Knight, Tomb 7,
Monte Alban, Oaxaca, Mexico.   *b*) Gold figure of the Aztec king,
Tizoc, Texcoco, Mexico.   *c*) Cast gold pectoral with fantastic
animal, Costa Rica.

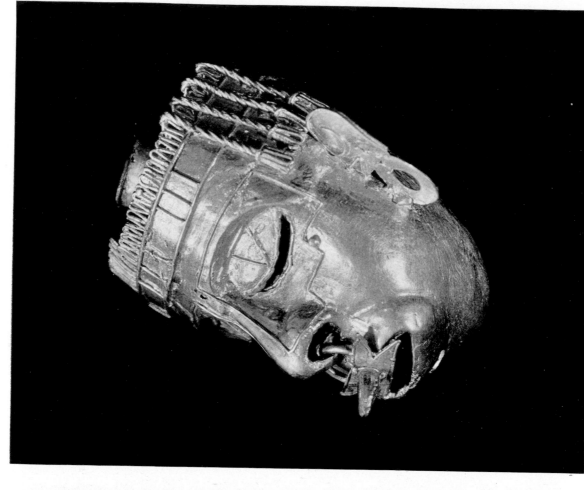

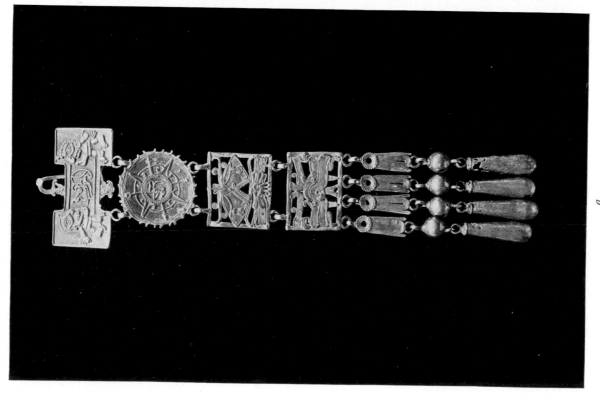

PLATE 232. ©. *a*) Gold pendant made up of seven symbolic elements. *b*) Small gold mask of Xipe-Totec. Tomb 7, Monte Alban.

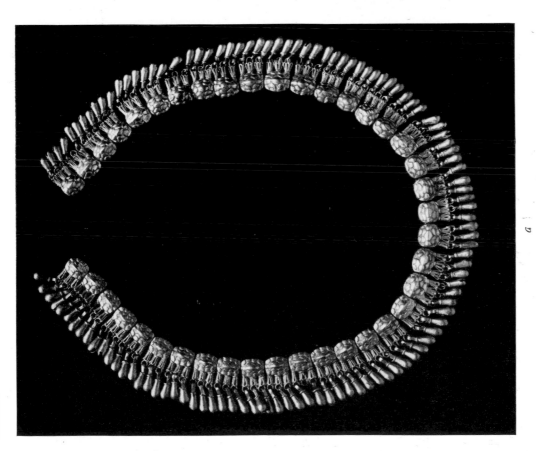

PLATE 233. ©. *a*) Gold necklace, Oaxaca. *b*) Small gold plaque, Vera Cruz.

*a*

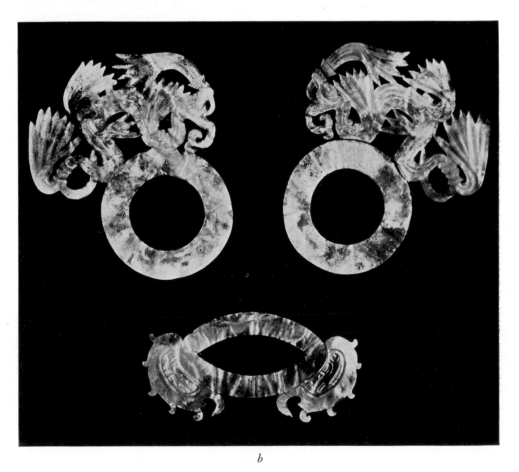

*b*

PLATE 234.   ©.   *a*) Gold solar disk in repoussé, Texmilincan, Guerrero.   *b*) Gold frames for eyes
and mouth from a mask, Sacred Well, Chichen Itzá.

JADE AND OTHER SEMIPRECIOUS STONES

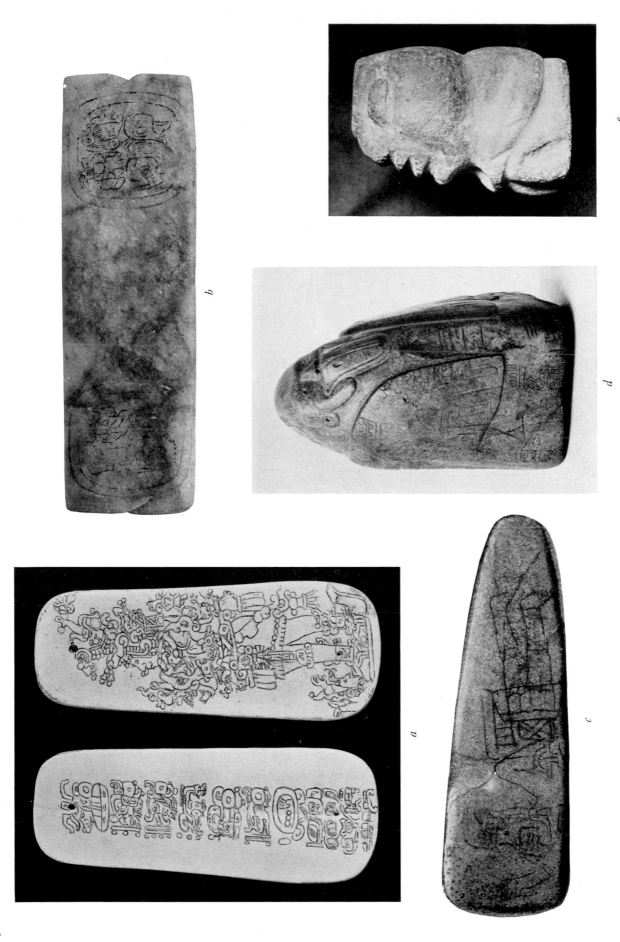

PLATE 235.  ©.  *a*) The Leyden plaque, Guatemala.  *b*) Bar bead with Maya glyphs.  *c*) Celt-shaped "palette" with incision, Mexico.  *d*) The Tuxtla statuette, Mexico.  *e*) Light-colored stone statuette, Guatemala.

JADE

MAYA AREA

PLATE 236. ©. *a*) Early stone stela (Stela I), Copan, Honduras. *b* and *c*) Bar pectorals with human figures, Kaminaljuyú and Quiriguá, Guatemala. *d*) Plaque showing similarity to *fig. a*, San Salvador.

PLATE 237.  ©.  *a*) Large pendant, Costa Rica.  *b*) Pectorals, Venezuela.   Small pendants:
*c* and *d*) provenience unknown;   *e*) Zacualpa, Guatemala;   *f*) Oaxaca, Mexico.

*a*

*b*

*c*

*d*

PLATE 238.  ©.  *a*) Serpentine plaque representing Tlaloc, Mexico.  *b*) Large pendant, found near
Teotihuacan.  *c*) Maya plaque.  *d*) Mexican pendant.

PLATE 239.  ⓒ.   Small Mexican pendants showing:   *a* and *b*) figures;   *c* and *d*) heads in frontal view;
*e* and *f*) heads in profile.

PLATE 240. ©. *a* and *b*) Mexican pendants, with figures engaged in some activity. *c* and *d*) Mayoid plaques, with seated dignitaries. *e* and *f*) Maya plaques, with seated dignitaries.

JADE

PLATE 241. ©. Small Maya and Mayoid heads: *a*, *e*, and *g*) provenience unknown; *b*) Palenque, Mexico; *c* and *h*) Guatemalan highlands; *d*) Chichen Itzá, Mexico; *f*) Oaxaca?, Mexico.

*a*                                              *b*

*c*                                              *d*

PLATE 242. ©. Statuettes: *a* and *b*) Copan, Honduras; *c*) Uaxactun, Guatemala,
*by special permission of Carnegie Institution of Washington;* *d*) green diorite, Mexico.

PLATE 243.  Ⓒ.  *a*) Serpentine statuette, Vera Cruz.  *b*) Tiger-mouth figure,
Puebla.  *c* and *d*) Olmec types.

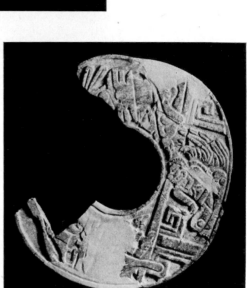

*c*

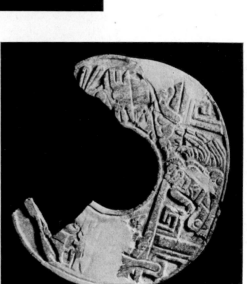

*b*

*a*

PLATE 244. ©. *a* and *b*) Crystal bead necklace and fragment of carved jade disk, Chichen Itzá. *c*) Jade beads and pendant, Mexico.

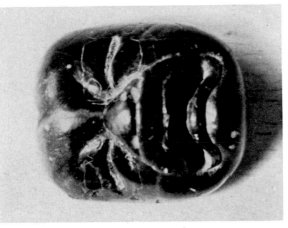

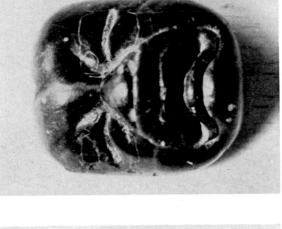

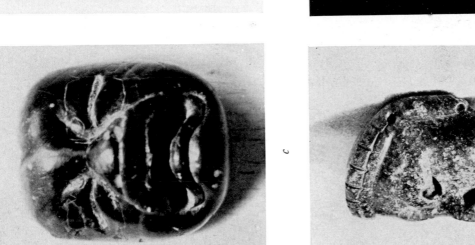

PLATE 245. ©. Small pendants in the form of human heads showing stylistic variations: *a, b, c, d,* and *f* ) provenience unknown, Mexico; *e* ) Palenque, Mexico; *g* ) El Salvador; *h* ) Yucatan, Mexico.

*a*

*b*

PLATE 246.   ©.   *a*) Olmec pectoral.   *b*) Olmec plaque.

*a*

*b*

*c*

*d*

PLATE 247. ©. Small heads. Mexico.

*a*

*b*

*c*

*d*

PLATE 248.  ©.  Larger stone masks:  *a*) Aztec;  *b*) Totonac? with Olmec traits;  *c* and *d*) Totonac.

*a*

*b*

*c*

*d*

PLATE 249.   ©.   Large stone masks:   *a* and *d*) Toltec;   *b*) showing Toltec influence;   *c*) style indefinite.

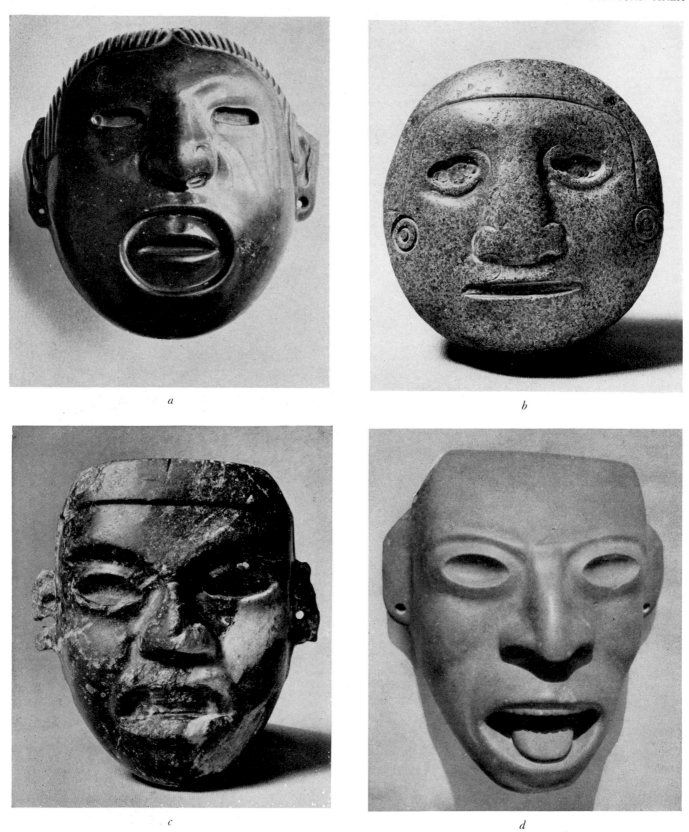

PLATE 250.  ©.  *a*) Black stone mask of Xipe-Totec, Oaxaca.  *b*) Round mask, provenience unknown.  *c*) Toltec mask.  *d*) Large Toltec? serpentine mask.

PLATE 251. ©. *a*) Jaguar head, Piedras Negras, Guatemala. *b*) Obsidian monkey head, Puebla, Mexico. *c*) Small mask, El Salvador. *d*) Amphibian, provenience unknown. *e*) Fan handle, Monte Alban, Mexico. *f*) Hand, Ulua Valley, Honduras.

*a*                                                 *b*

*c*                                                 *d*

PLATE 252. ©. Standing human figures, Mexico: *a*) Puebla; *b*) dark stone, provenience unknown; *c* and *d*) side and frontal views, light green jade, with Olmec traits, provenience unknown.

*a*

*b*

*c*

*d*

PLATE 253. ©. Seated human figures: *a*) dark stone, provenience unknown; *b*) pyrite, provenience unknown; *c*) dark jade, Ulua Valley, Honduras; *d*) light green jade, with Olmec traits, provenience unknown.

PLATE 254. ©. *a*) Vessel representing Tlaloc, the Rain-god. *b*) Statue of Toci, Mother of the Gods. Mexico.

*a*

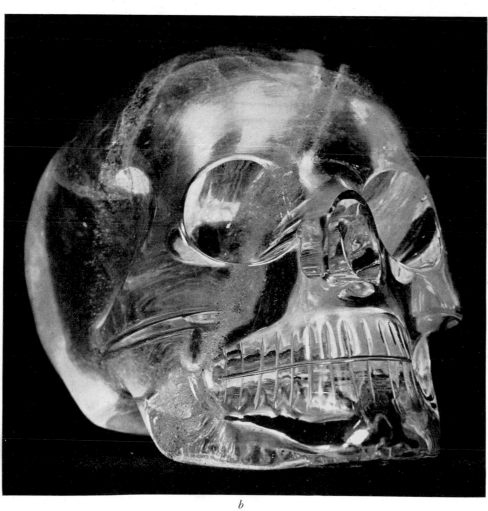

*b*

PLATE 255.   ©.   Objects of rock crystal, Mexico:   *a*) goblet, Monte Alban;   *b*) skull.

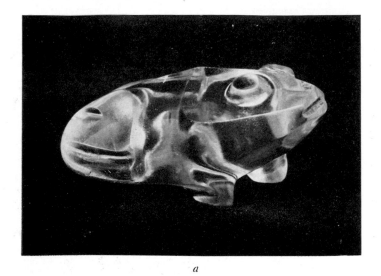

*a*

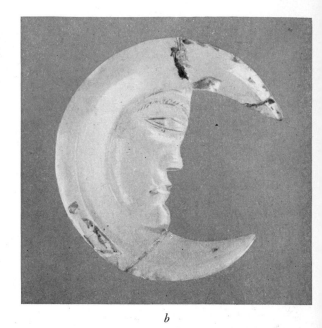

*b*

*c*

*d*

PLATE 256. ©. *a*) Rock crystal frog, Mexico. *b*) Rock crystal man in the moon, Mexico. *c*) Obsidian model of a temple-base, Mexico. *d*) Eccentric flint in human shape, Maya?.

*a*          *b*

*c*          *d*

PLATE 257.   Ⓒ.   Onyx vases:   *a*) Monte Alban, Mexico;   *c* and *d*) Isla de los Sacrificios, Vera Cruz, Mexico.   *b*) Small jade vase, El Salvador.

*a*

*b*

*c*

PLATE 258. Ⓒ. *a* and *b*) Mochica statuettes of turquoise and silver, demonstrating uniformity of iconography, North Coast of Peru. *c*) Small turquoise vase with Chavin traits.

# MURALS AND MANUSCRIPTS

*a*

*b*

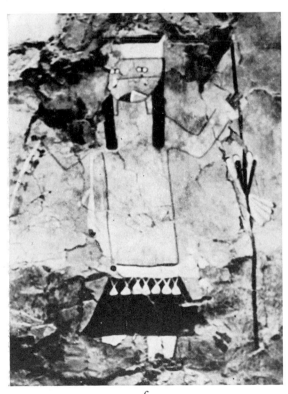

*c*

PLATE 259. ©. *a* and *b*) Murals, Awatovi, Arizona.
*c*) Fragment of mural, Kuaua, New Mexico.

*a*

*b*

PLATE 260.   ⓒ.   Sections of murals in the Temple of Agriculture, Teotihuacan.

*a*

*b*

PLATE 261.   ©.   *a*) Section of a carved and painted wall, Temple of the Bas-Relief, Chichen Itzá.
*b*) Mural, Altar A, Tizatlan.   Mexico.

*a*

*b*

PLATE 262. Ⓒ. *a*) Wall-painting from early Maya structure B-XIII, Uaxactun, Guatemala. *By special permission of Carnegie Institution of Washington and A. Ledyard Smith.* *b*) Wall-painting from Edifice 3, Chacmultun, Yucatan, Mexico. Note stylistic differences in these pure Maya murals when compared with the fragments below from the Mexican period of Chichen Itzá.

*a*

*b*

*c*

PLATE 263. ©. *a*) Seacoast village scene, Temple of the Warriors, Chichen Itzá, Mexico. *b*) Scene with plant and animal life, and *c*) scene with warriors. Temple of the Tigers, Chichen Itzá.

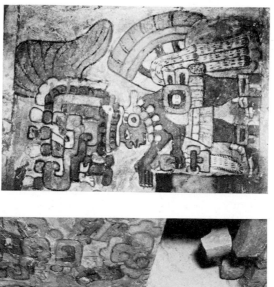

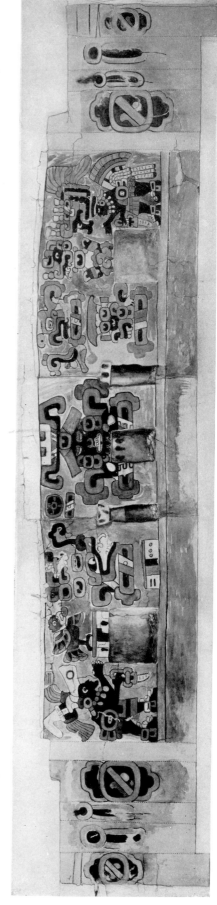

*c*

*b*

*a*

*d*

PLATE 264. ⓒ. *b*) Interior of Zapotec Tomb 104, Monte Alban. *a* and *c*) Details. Figures of Xipe-Totec and the Maize-god. *d*) Unrolled design of entire mural.

*a*

*b*

*c*

*d*

PLATE 265.  Ⓒ.    *a* and *b*) Details of murals at Mitla, Oaxaca, and Tulum, Quintana Roo, Mexico.
*c*) Section of Maya codex (Dresdensis).    *d*) Section of Aztec codex (Borbonicus).

PLATE 266.  ©.  Page from the Maya Codex Dresdensis.

*a*

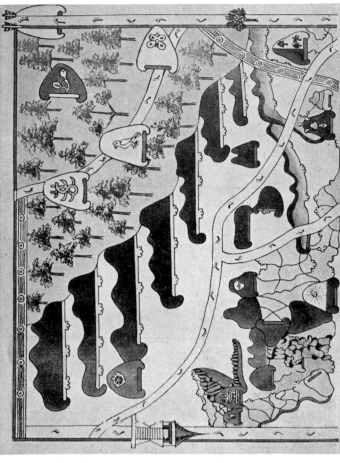

*c*

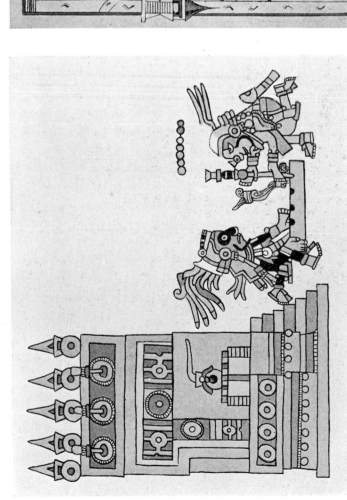

*b*

PLATE 267. ©. *a*) Unfolded pages of Aztec codex (Vaticanus B). *b*) Detail from Zapotec codex (Colombino). *c*) Section of Aztec map.

PLATE 268. ©. *a*) Scene from post-Columbian Aztec codex (Magliabecchiano). *b*) Detail from post-Columbian Aztec codex (Mendoza). *c*) Fiesta scene from pre-Columbian Aztec codex (Borbonicus).

PLATE 269.  ©.  Page from the Tribute Roll of Montezuma.

PLATE 270. ©. Vignettes from Sahagun's codex (Florentino): *a*) farmers storing corn; *b*) four judges supervising execution of malefactors by noose and club—note different fabrics; *c, d,* and *e*) spider, butterfly and grasshopper; *f*) Spaniards landing at Vera Cruz—note delineation of animals; *g*) market scene; *h*) the *conquistadores* on their way to the capital meeting a native deputation—note volcanoes in the background.

# MISCELLANEOUS APPLIED ARTS

*a*

*b*

PLATE 271.   ⓒ.   *a*) Wooden mask representing antlered human head, Oklahoma.
*b*) Wooden mask of a doe, Florida.

WOOD

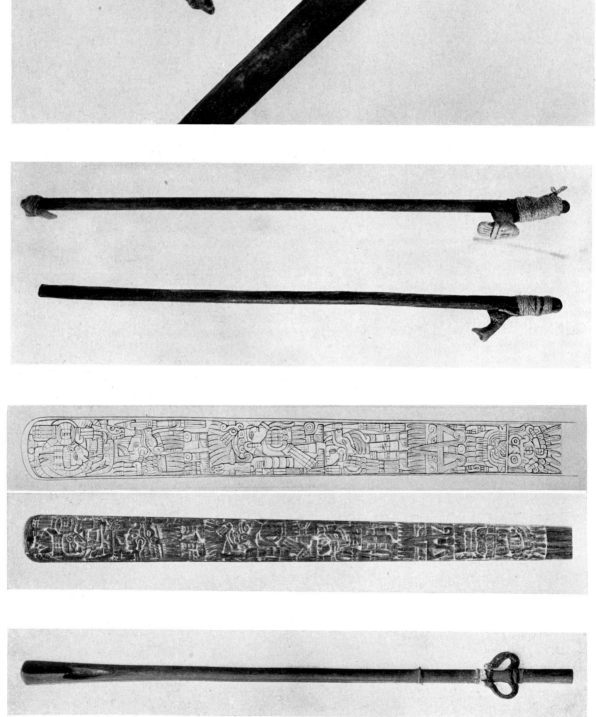

PLATE 272. ©. Wooden spear-throwers, or *atlatls*: *a*) Southwest; *b*) Mexico; *c*) copy of design; *d*) Peru; *e*) detail of hand grip, with bone figure playing panpipes, Peru.

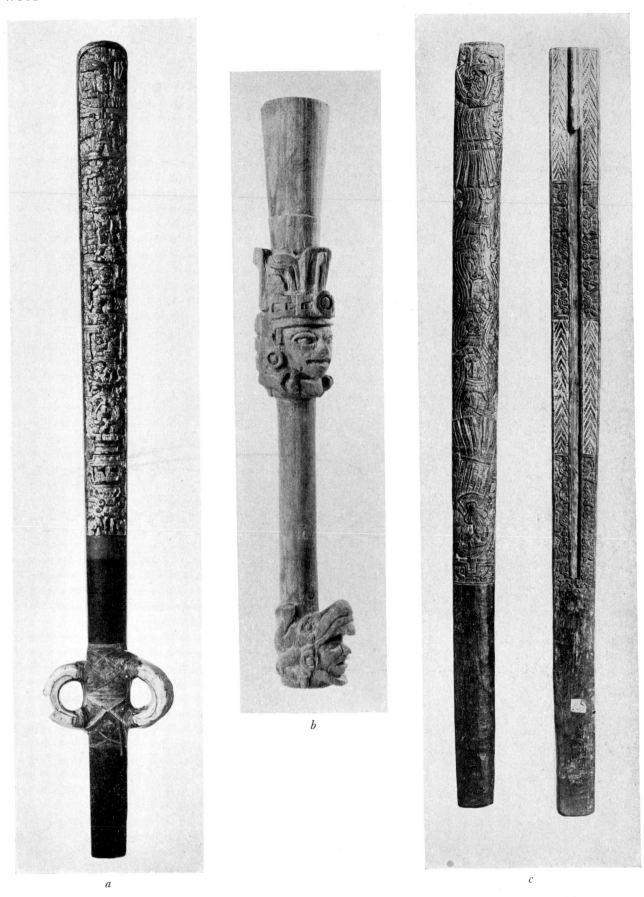

PLATE 273.  ⓒ.  *a*) Carved and gilded ceremonial *atlatl*, Mexico.  *b*) Top of wooden
ceremonial staff, Sacred Well, Chichen Itzá.  *c*) Carved and painted *atlatls*, Oaxaca.

PLATE 274.  ©.  Carved wood lintel, Tikal, Guatemala.

*a*                                                              *b*

*c*

PLATE 275.   ©.   *a*) Carved top of staff or paddle, Ica.   *b*) Pendant of a coca bag, Ica.   *c*) Wooden spoons
with carved handles, Coast Tiahuanaco.

*c*

*f*

*b*

*e*

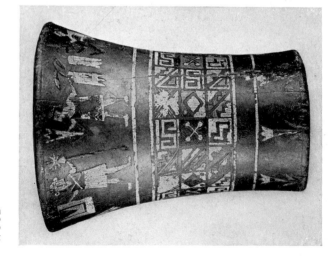

*a*

*d*

PLATE 276. ©. *Keros*, or wooden cups with lacquer-like finish, late Inca and post-Conquest.

*a*

*b*

PLATE 277.  ©.  *a*) Seat supported by jaguars, lacquer-like finish, Inca.  *b*) Carved
beam of a scale, Chimu?.

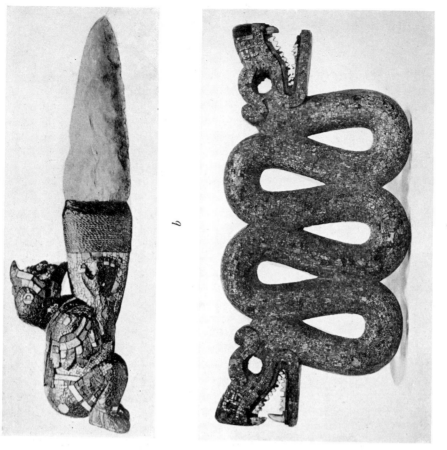

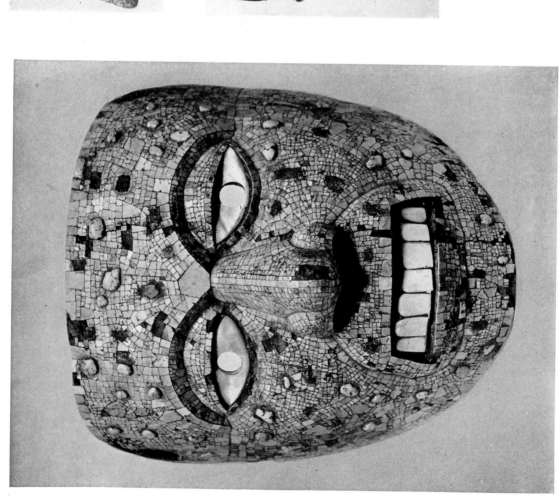

PLATE 278. ©. Objects incrusted with turquoise mosaic, Mexico: *a*) mask of Quetzalcoatl?; *b*) ceremonial knife with Eagle Knight; *c*) ornament with double-headed serpent.

PLATE 279. ⓒ. *a*) Wooden helmet with mosaic incrustation. *b*) Wooden shield with ceremonial scene in turquoise. Mexico.

*a*

*b*

PLATE 280. ©. Shell gorgets: *a*) Tennessee; *c*) Oklahoma. *b*) Conch with incised decoration and inset showing bird-man design, Oklahoma.

*c*

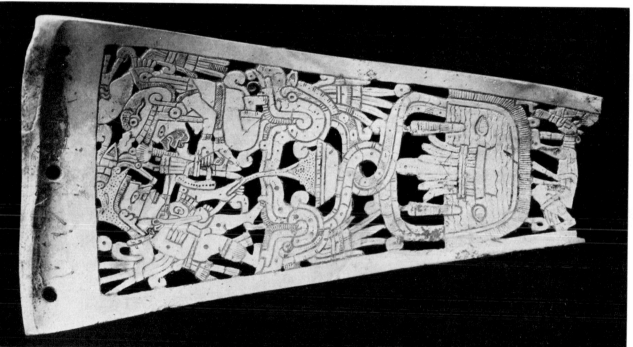

*b*

*a*

PLATE 281. ©. *a* and *c*) Perforated shell gorgets, Georgia. *b*) Perforated shell ornament, Vera Cruz, Mexico.

SHELL

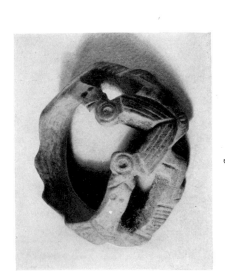

PLATE 282. ©. *a*) Hohokam ring of glycimeris shell, Arizona. *b*) Xipe-Totec mask of reddish shell, Mexico. *c*) Mother-of-pearl pendant with seated Maya warrior, Tula, Mexico.

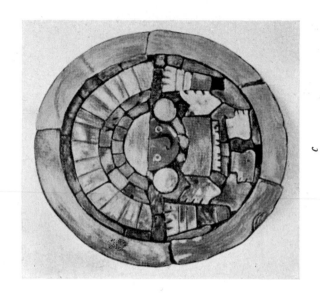

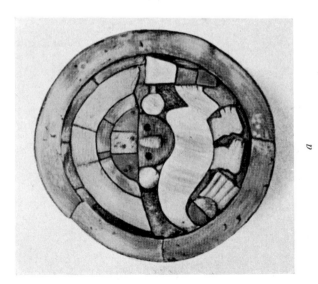

*c*

*b*

*a*

PLATE 283. Ⓒ. Chimu shell mosaic-work:  *a* and *c*) earplugs;  *b*) cup with wooden base.

BONE

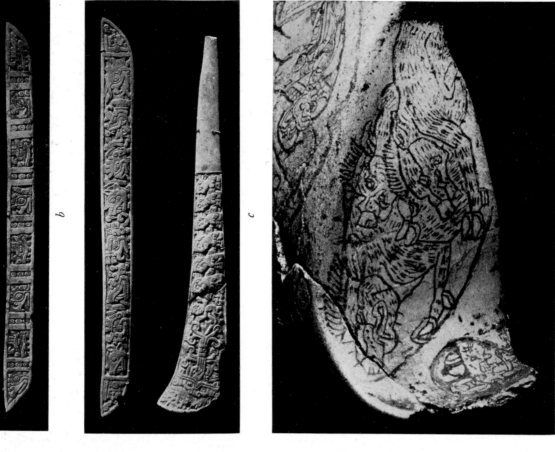

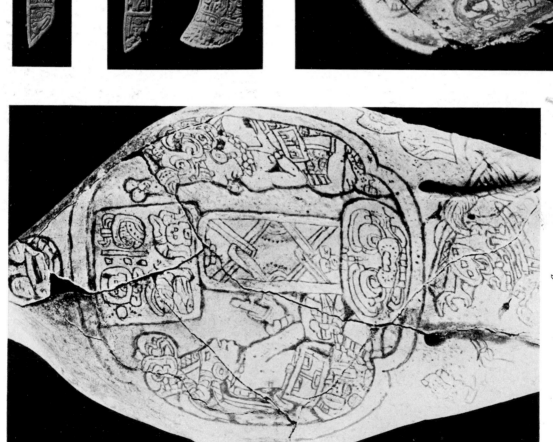

PLATE 284.  ©.  *a* and *d* ) Details of an incised peccary skull, Copan, Honduras.  *b* and *c* ) Jaguar bone with glyphic carving, Monte Alban, Mexico.

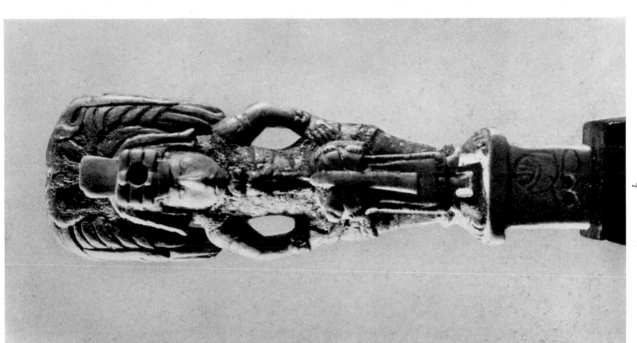

PLATE 285. ©. *a*) Hohokam bone awl handle with mountain sheep, Arizona. *b*) Maya priest carved of jaguar bone, probably top of a staff, provenience unknown. *c*) Back of figure.

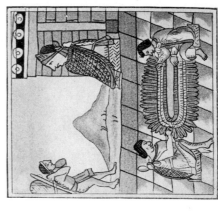

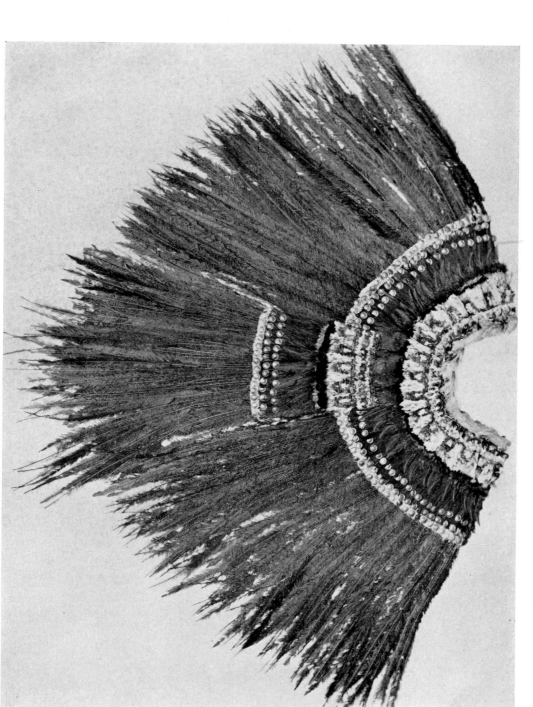

PLATE 286.  ©.  *a*)  Aztec feather headdress or cloak, gift of Montezuma to Charles V.  *b*)  Vignette from Sahagun's codex (Florentino) showing craftsmen making feather-work.

*c*

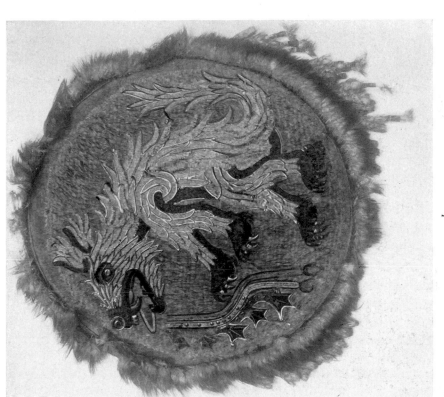

*b*

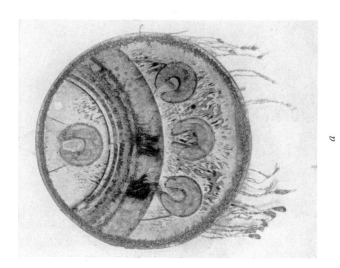

*a*

PLATE 287. ©. *a*) Aztec feather shield mounted on jaguar skin. *b*) Aztec œremonial shield of feathers with gold outlining, showing the coyote Fire-god, and *c*) Aztec feather standard with fire-flower, both gifts of Montezuma to Charles V.

PLATE 288. ©. Mitre and infula of Mexican feather-work, post-Columbian.

*a*

*b*

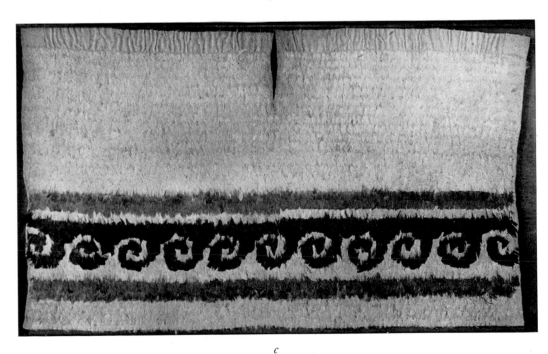

*c*

PLATE 289. ©. *a*) Feather fan with woven framework, Central Coast? of Peru.
*b*) Pair of earplugs decorated with feather-work, Ica. *c*) Feather poncho, Chimu.

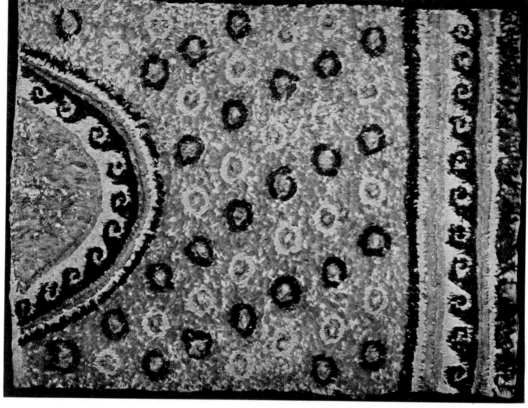

PLATE 290. ⓒ. *a*) Feather poncho with birds and feline figures, Ica. *b*) Feather poncho with geometric design, Chimu.

*a*

*b*

# FACETS OF DAILY LIFE

a

b

c

PLATE 291. ©. a) Agricultural terraces, Andean highlands, Peru. b) Vignette from Sahagun's codex (Florentino), showing cultivation of corn with planting stick, Mexico. c) Modern Hopi Indian planting corn, using similar implement, Arizona.

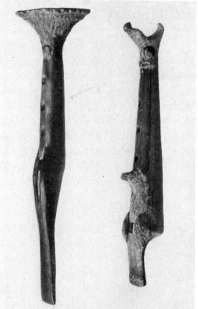

*b*

*e*

*a*

*d*

*c*

PLATE 292. ©. *a*) Aztec stone drum. *b*) Aztec wooden drum. *c*) Vignette from Sahagun's codex (Florentino), showing merrymakers with two types of drums and rattles. *d*) Pottery flutes, Mexico. *e*) Pottery figurines of musicians and chiefs, Monte Alban.

*a*

*b*

*c*

PLATE 293. ©. *a*) Wooden *teponaztlis,* or two-toned drums, carved in
relief, and drumstick. *b* and *c*) Same type of instrument, carved in human and
animal shapes. Mexico.

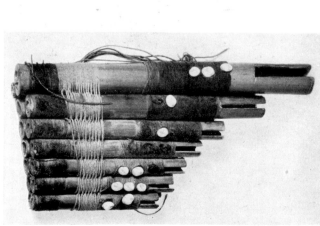

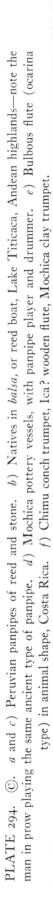

PLATE 294. ©. *a* and *c*) Peruvian panpipes of reed and stone. *b*) Natives in *balsa*, or reed boat, Lake Titicaca, Andean highlands—note the man in prow playing the same ancient type of panpipe. *d*) Mochica pottery vessels, with panpipe player and drummer. *e*) Bulbous flute (ocarina type) in animal shape, Ica? wooden flute, Mochica clay trumpet. *f*) Chimu conch trumpet, Costa Rica.

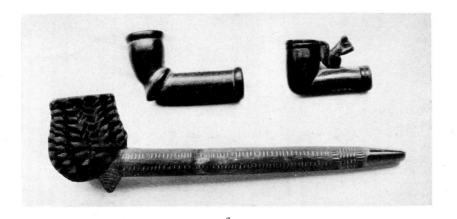

*a*

*b*

*c*

*d*

*e*

*f*

PLATE 295. ©. *a*) Universal types of pipes: top row, stone, Georgia; corncob shape, pottery, Mexico. Mound Builder stone effigy pipes: *b*) human, Ohio; *c*) owl, Illinois; *d*) squirrel, Ohio; *e*) monster, Alabama; *f*) duck and owl, Virginia.

PLATE 296. Ⓒ. Mound Builder stone effigy pipes: *a*) dog; *b*) otter with fish; *d*) hawk; *e*) crane; *f*) duck on back of fish. All from Ohio. *c*) Swimming duck, Kentucky.

*a*

*b*

*c*

PLATE 297.  ©.  *a* and *c*) Pottery effigy pipes in human shape.  *b*) Pottery incense burner, with human
figure used for decoration.  Mexico.

*a*

*b*                                    *c*

PLATE 298.  ©.   *a*) Obsidian mirror with gilded wood frame, showing reflection of effigy vessel, Vera Cruz?, Mexico.  *b*) Chimu? pyrite mirror with carved and painted wood frame, coast of Peru.  *c*) Carved and painted wood back of a Chimu mirror, Lambayeque, Peru.

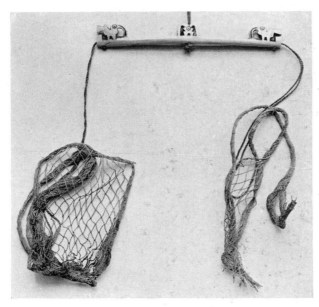

*a*

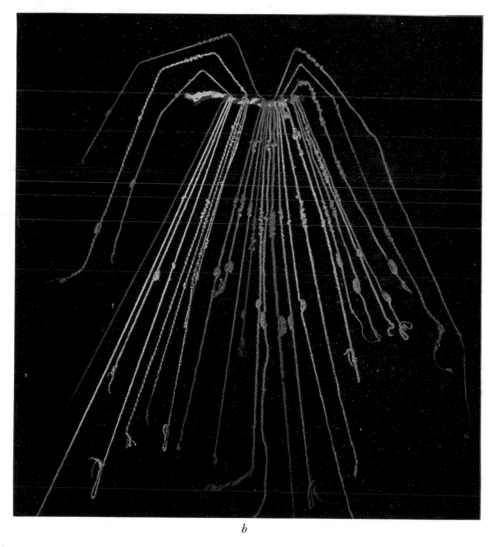

*b*

PLATE 299.  ©.  *a*) Chimu balance scale with beam of carved bone and netted bags.  *b*) *Quipu,* or
knot record, Chancay.  Peru.

*a*

*b*

PLATE 300.  Ⓒ.  *a*) Airview of jungle bush, showing the course of two intersecting Maya
roads, Yucatan, Mexico.  *b*) Airview of remnants of Chimu highways and ruin in coastal sands,
Chicama Valley, Peru.

*a*

*b*

PLATE 301. ©. *a*) Airview of Pueblo ruins, Aztec, New Mexico. *b*) Airview of ancient Maya
walled seacoast city, Tulum, Mexico.

*a*

*b*

PLATE 302.   ©.   *a*) Airview of the Citadel, with Quetzalcoatl Temple, Teotihuacan, Mexico.   *b*) Airview of a section of the ancient Chimu capital, Chan-Chan, Peru.

a

b

c

PLATE 303.  ©.  *a*) Partly restored antechamber and entrance to Maya sweat bath, Chichen Itzá, Mexico.
*b*) Restored section, showing vapor vent.  *c*) Ruins of an Inca reservoir and water distributing system,
Sacsahuaman, Peru.

PLATE 304.  ©.  Stairway to the main entrance, El Castillo, Chichen Itzá, Mexico; inset: wooden pole with hewn footholds, a primitive ladder still in use, border region of Guatemala and El Salvador.

*a*

*b*

PLATE 305.   ©.   *a*) Ruined east stairway, Temple of the Dwarf, Uxmal, Mexico.   *b*) Stairway
connecting different levels, Machu Picchu, Peru.

*a*

*b*

PLATE 306. ⓒ. Phuyu Pata Marka, or the City above the Clouds, Peru, near Machu Picchu: *a*) view from the northeast, showing water channels and basins in foreground; *b*) view from the northwest.

# CATALOGUE OF ILLUSTRATIONS

# Catalogue of Illustrations

This compilation contains data, measurements, and various credits not included in the text or captions. Measurements denote height unless otherwise stated. When a museum or a collector owns the piece and has also furnished the photograph of it, the name is given only once. The following abbreviations have been used for names which occur most frequently.

| | |
|---|---|
| AMNH. | American Museum of Natural History, New York |
| BG. | Brummer Gallery, Inc., New York |
| CIW. | Carnegie Institution of Washington, Washington, D. C. |
| DO. | Dumbarton Oaks Collection, Washington, D.C. |
| EZK. | Elisabeth Zulauf Kelemen |
| FAM. | Fogg Art Museum, Cambridge, Mass. |
| FM. | Field Museum, Chicago, Ill. |
| INAH. | Instituto Nacional de Antropología e Historia, Mexico, D.F. |
| JW. | John Wise, Ltd., New York |
| LA. | Laboratory of Anthropology, Santa Fé, N.M. |
| LAM. | Los Angeles Museum of History, Science, and Art, Los Angeles, Calif. |
| M. | Museum |
| MAG. | Museo de Arqueología, Guatemala |
| MAI. | Museum of the American Indian, Heye Foundation, New York |
| MAL. | Museo Nacional de Arqueología, Lima, Peru |
| MARI. | Middle American Research Institute, Tulane University, New Orleans, La. |
| MFA. | Museum of Fine Arts, Boston, Mass. |
| MH. | Musée de l'Homme, Paris, France |
| MN. | Museo Nacional de Arqueología, Historia y Etnografia, Mexico, D.F. |
| MVBG. | Museum für Völkerkunde, Berlin, Germany |
| MVBS. | Museum für Völkerkunde, Basle, Switzerland |
| MVVA. | Museum für Völkerkunde, Vienna, Austria |
| OSM. | Ohio State Museum, Columbus, Ohio |
| Ph. | Photograph |
| PM. | Peabody Museum of Harvard University, Cambridge, Mass. |
| RC. | Rossbach Collection, Chichicastenango, Guatemala |
| TM. | Textile Museum of the District of Columbia, Washington, D.C. |
| UCAL. | University of California Museum, Berkeley, Calif. |
| UMP. | The University Museum, Philadelphia, Pa. |
| USNM. | United States National Museum, Washington, D.C. |

# Architecture

# ARCHITECTURE

# CATALOGUE OF ILLUSTRATIONS

# Sculpture

# SCULPTURE

90 Bust of the Maize-god, Copan, Honduras. 36 in. British **M**.

91 Plastic decorations on the bases of buildings. *a*) Palace group, Palenque, Chiapas, Mexico, dated early 6th century. Ph: Garcia. *b*) From an early structure, but later used as building material, Monte Alban, Oaxaca, Mexico. Ph: EZK. *c*) Acanceh, northern Yucatan, Mexico, dated early 8th century. Ph: PM. *d*) Temple of the Warriors, Chichen Itzá, Yucatan. Ph: CIW.

92 *a*) Detail of mural, Temple of Chacmool, Chichen Itzá, Yucatan, Mexico, showing warrior seated on jaguar throne. 14¼ x 11 in. After a water color by Ann A. Morris. *b*) Jaguar throne from inner temple, El Castillo, Chichen Itzá. 33 in. long and 27 high. Phs: CIW.

93 *a*) Carved columns, Temple of the Atlantean Columns, No. 2, Chichen Itzá, Yucatan, Mexico. Ph: CIW. *b*) Chacmool from Chichen Itzá. Nearly 5 ft. long. MN.

94 Sculptured marble vases, Ulua Valley, Honduras. *a*) Body, about 4 in. BG. *b*) 7⅜ in. MARI. *c*) 6¼ in. Pierre Matisse Gallery, N. Y. *d*) About 5 in. UMP.

95 Sculptured marble vases, Ulua Valley, Honduras. *a*) 9⅝ in. UMP. *b*) About 2 in. BG.

### INTERLYING AREA

96 Seated stone figures. *a*) Chichicastenango, Guatemala. 11 in. RC. Ph:EZK. *b*) Rio Frio, Costa Rica. Property of Dr. S. W. Fernberger. Ph: UMP.

97 Sculptured "axes": *a*) Putulul, near Atitlán, Guatemala. 12 in. *b*) Asunción Mita, Guatemala. 11 in. Both at MAG. Phs: EZK.
Stone figures: *c*) East Costa Rica. Nearly 50 in. AMNH. *d*) Dual Officiants. About 14 in. Museo Nacional, San José, Costa Rica.

98 Sculptured *metates,* or grinding stones. *a*) Found at Santa Lucia Cotzumalhuapa, Guatemala, but Chorotegan in type. 47 in. long and 21 high; roller, 34 in. long. UMP. *b*) Costa Rica. 34 in. long and 9 in. high. Chiriqui culture. AMNH. *c*) Pacific coast, Nicaragua. 29 in. long and 12 high. Gift of Govt. of Nicaragua to USNM.

### ANDEAN AREA

99 *a*) Monolith E, Cerro Sechin, Casma Valley, North Coast of Peru. About 8 ft. Museo de la Universidad, Lima, Peru. *b*) Stela Raimondi, Chavin de Huántar, Peru. 6½ ft. MAL. *c*) Giant statue, Tiahuanaco, Bolivia. Nearly 24 ft. Ph: Grace Line.

100 Carved stone bowls. *a*) Chavin de Huántar. 6½ in. high and 13 long. UMP. *b*) Highland Inca. 5 in. high and 26 long. UMP.

# Pottery

PLATE

### THE SOUTHWEST

101 Pottery shapes from Arizona. *a*) Coiled-ware pot, Apache Co. 13 in. MAI. *b*) Corrugated bowl with incised decoration. AMNH. *c*) Three painted bowls, the first and third from eastern Arizona, 9th century, and the second from north central Arizona, 13th century. LA. *d*) Bowl with figures, Linden. 4 in. high and 8¾ in diameter. USNM. *e*) Hohokam incense burner. LAM.

102 Water jars, or *ollas*. *a*) Say-od-nee-chee, Ariz. Two larger, 16 in. PM. *b*) Black-on-white, Mesa Verde, Colo., 12th century. Denver Art Museum. *c*) Black-on-white, Socorro, central New Mexico, about 13th century. 15 in. high and 15 in diameter. LA.

103 Various painted pottery. *a*) Apache Co., Ariz., 10-12th century. 3 in. high and 9½ in diameter. USNM. *b*) Sityatki, Ariz., 14th century. 3½ in. high and 10½ in diameter. USNM. *c*) "Four-mile polychrome," east central Arizona, 14th century. Diameter, about 10 in. LA. *d*) Deming, N. M. 4½ in. high and 11½ in diameter. USNM. *e*) Pueblo III water carrier or canteen, Mesa Verde, Colo., U. S. Dept. of Interior, Park Service. *f*) Gray-ware water carrier, Ariz. 8 in. MAI.

104 *a*) Three Pueblo mugs, black-on-white, Navaho Canyon, Ariz. and Colo., about 11th century. UMP. *b*) Double jar, Mesa Verde, Colo., about 13th century.

PLATE

University of Colorado, Boulder. Ph: Earl Morris. *c*) Tularosa dipper, N. M. AMNH.

105 Various types of black-and-white and colored wares. *a*) Western New Mexico, the first dated about 9th century, and the second and third, 13th century. LA. *b*) Pueblo III kiva jars, Mesa Verde, Colo. U. S. Dept. of Interior, Park Service. *c*) Sityatki, Ariz., 15th century. 4 in. high and 7 in diameter. USNM. *d*) Chihuahua polychrome, north Chihuahua, Mexico, 15th century. 7 or 8 in. LA.

106 Bowls from Mimbres Valley, N. M., averaging about 10 in. in diameter. *a, c,* and *e*) PM. *b* and *d*) about 1100. University of Colorado, Boulder. Ph: Earl Morris. *e*) Buffalo Museum of Science.

107 Bowls from Mimbres Valley, N. M. PM.

### MISCELLANEOUS U. S. A.

108 *a*) Painted water bottle, Ark. PM. *b*) Painted water bottle, Ark. 10¼ in. FM. *c*) Mound Builder brown-ware incised bowl, Onachita Parish, La. 2¾ in. MAI. *d*) Brown-ware burial urn with stamped decoration, Liberty Co., Ga. 17 in. MAI.

109 *a*) Precipitation jar, probably used in salt making, near Saline Springs, Kimmswick, Mo. 18½ in. long. PM. *b*) Two black-ware bottles, Ark., 7 and 6⅛ in. respectively. MAI. *c*) Burnished horned snake effigy bowl, Ark. About 8 in. FM.

*d*) Mound Builder incised brown-ware bottle, Onachita Parish, La. 7 in. MAI.

#### MEXICAN AREA

110 Early shapes in pottery. *a*) Early Zapotec jar with two spout handles, Monte Alban, Oaxaca. 15 in. *b*) Toltec jar with polychrome on stucco, Teotihuacan, near Mexico, D. F. *c*) Toltec cinerary urn and lid, with cut-in decoration and engraving, Teotihuacan. 9½ in. All MN.

111 Pitchers: *a*) Toluca Valley, Mexico. About 11 in. Matlatzincan-Aztec. FM. *b*) 8½ in. Mixtec. MN. *c*) Puebla. British M.
Tripods from the Zapotec-Mixtec region: *d*) Mitla, Oaxaca. 7½ in. FM. *e*) Oaxaca. Under 4 in. Mixtec. FM. *f*) Vase with stellar decoration, Oaxaca. Mixtec. NM.

112 Tarascan figures in clay. *a*) Woman with *metate*. 4½ in. F. Davis Coll., Mexico. Ph: EZK. *b*) Seated figure, Jalisco, before 1200. 28 in. FM. *c*) Group of dancing women. Diameter, about 9 in. MN.

113 *a*) Tarascan mother and child. MN. *b*) Aztec? miniature warrior. 2 in. F. Davis Coll., Mexico. Ph: EZK. *c*) Figure lying bound on a couch, Mexico. MH. *d*) "Pretty lady," Valley of Mexico. 4¼ in. R. Weitlaner Coll., Tacubaya. Ph: EZK. *e*) "Pretty ladies," the first, over 5 in. F. Davis Coll., Mexico. Phs: EZK.

114 Pottery types from Colima, Michoacan, Mexico. *a*) Recumbent dog. 7½ in. long. FM. *b*) Dog and baby, 10½ and 11 in. respectively. Metropolitan Museum of Art on loan to AMNH. *c*) Burnished pottery dog. About 11 in. high and 15½ long. FM. *d*) Tripod jar. MAI.

115 *a*) Tarascan warrior with club or spear-thrower. About 2 ft. BG. *b*) Tarascan warrior with club. MN. Ph: FAM. *c*) Small standing figure, Chiapas, Mexico. About 6 in. AMNH. *d*) Seated figure, central Vera Cruz. 13½ in. AMNH.

116 *a* and *b*) Cholula plates from near Puebla. Aztec, mid-14th century. Dr. S. K. Loth-rop Coll. Ph: Brooklyn M. *c*) Mixtec? serpent effigy jar. Over 8 in. BG. *d*) Huaxtec? cylindrical vase with "sgrafitto" decoration. About 15 in. high and 8 in diameter. MARI.

117 Clay heads from different cultures. *a*) Early period pottery head, Type Di, Zacatenco, D.F. About 1¾ in. AMNH. *b*) Vera Cruz?. About 11 in. Cleveland Museum of Art. *c*) Figurine, Guadalajara, Jalisco. About 5 in. British M. *d*) Totonac laughing face, Vera Cruz. 6½ in. MAI. *e*) Vera Cruz?. About 8 in. BG.

118 *a*) Huaxtec figurine, Tempoal, Vera Cruz. 9⅜ in. AMNH. *b*) Masquette of moan bird, or Yucatecan screech owl, Tuxtla district, Vera Cruz. 6 in. UMP. *c*) Pottery whistle, central Vera Cruz. AMNH. *d*) Leaf-nose bat as God of Death, Tuxtla district, Vera Cruz. 2 in. high and 3½ long. UMP.

119 Large Aztec terra-cotta figures. *a*) Wearing flayed skin, found in a cave at Coatlinchan, Mexico. About life size. AMNH. *b*) Warrior, provenience unknown. About 5½ ft. MN.

120 Zapotec Messenger Dogs of the Gods, effigy urns, near Guila, Oaxaca. 19¾ and 16½ in. respectively. UMP.

121 Effigy funerary urns and incense burners, Oaxaca. *a*) Seated jaguar, Zimatlan. MVBG. *b*) Standing figure, Tenexpa. UMP. *c*) Zapotec sacerdote, *incensario*, Monte Alban II. 32 in. MN.

122 Zapotec incense burners, Oaxaca. *a*) Rain-god, Atzompa. Monte Alban I. 33½ in. MN. *b*) Temple platform with figures. Monte Alban III. 16½ in. MN. *c*) Peripheral?. R. Weitlaner Coll., Tacubaya. Ph: EZK. *d*) 16 in. R. Dehesa Coll., Mexico. Ph: EZK.

123 Zapotec representations of human figures, Oaxaca. *a*) Brown-ware funerary urn, district of Choapan. 16¼ in. MAI. *b*) Funerary urn. 23½ in. MH. *c*) Brown-ware funerary urn, Etla district. 20 in. MAI. *d*) Seated figure. 13½ in. Oaxaca M. Ph: EZK.

# CATALOGUE OF ILLUSTRATIONS

139 *a*) Beaker with incised decoration, Guatemala?. Priv. Coll., San Francisco, Calif. Ph: UMP. *b*) Beaker with relief, incision, and painted decoration, Jutiapa, Guatemala. 9½ in. UMP. *c*) Buff beaker with glyphs in relief, Tonacatepeque, El Salvador. 9 in. Dr. Salazar Coll., San Salvador. *d*) Jar with incised glyphs and painted decoration, Ulua Valley, Honduras. 9 in. MAI.

140 Small flasks. *a*) El Progresso, Honduras. 3 in. MARI. *b*) Panchinalco, El Salvador. AMNH. *c*) El Salvador. 2½ in. long and 2½ in. high. Iméry Coll., San Salvador. *d*) El Salvador. 3½ in. Dr. Salazar Coll., San Salvador. *e*) Merida, Yucatan, Mexico. Ph: CIW. *f*) Dept. San Miguel, El Salvador. 5½ in. Zanotti Coll., El Salvador. *g*) Dept. San Miguel, El Salvador. 7 in. Dr. Salazar Coll. *h*) El Salvador. About 3 in. Iméry Coll. Phs: *c, f, g, h,* EZK.

141 Various shapes from the Guatemalan highlands. *a*) Double whistle jar with *pisote,* Kaminaljuyú. 8 in. MAG. *b*) Large tripod bowl with three human heads, Sololá?. Diameter, 16½ in. RC. *c*) Turkey effigy jar, Chorotegan type. 6 in. RC. *d*) Animal figure as sarcophagus, Nebaj. 3 ft. long. MAG. Phs: EZK.

142 *a*) Cylindrical jar with painted symbolic bird, El Salvador. 6½ in. Dr. Salazar Coll., San Salvador. Ph: EZK. *b*) Cylindrical tripod jar with plastic monkey head and painted decoration, El Salvador. 5½ in. Saundy Coll., Santa Técla. Ph: EZK. *c*) Vessel with painted decoration, Coclé, Panama. PM. *d*) Mayoid painted vase, with bat decoration. El Salvador. AMNH. *e*) Mayoid painted vase, Ulua Valley, Honduras. About 9 in. MARI.

143 Cylindrical vessels with animal handles, Honduras. *a*) Lake Yojoa. 10¼ in. MARI. *b*) Perales Calientas. About 12 in. Doris Stone Coll., New Orleans. Ph: MARI. *c*) Guanaja Island. 9½ in. MAI.

### INTERLYING AREA

144 Incense burner lids. *a*) Alta Verapaz, Guatemala. British M. *b*) Incense jar with lid, Ometepec Island, Managua, Nicaragua. Ph: CIW. *c*) Costa Rica. MAI.

145 *a*) Chorotegan animal effigy pot with negative painting, Nicoya, Costa Rica. 12½ in. Dr. S. K. Lothrop Coll., N. Y. Ph: FAM. *b*) Chorotegan negative-painted jar with rattle base, Costa Rica. 13¼ in. long and about 9 in diameter. MARI. *c*) Polychrome tripod bowl with rattle feet, Ometepec Island, Managua, Nicaragua. Property of Sgt. Asa Daniels, U. S. Marine Corps, on loan to LAM. *d*) Animal effigy jar with polychrome decoration, Zacualpa, Guatemala. 8 in. MAG. Ph: EZK.

146 Ceramic shapes, Coclé, Panama. *a*) Bottle, 8 in. Brooklyn M. *b*) "Goblet." *c*) Animal effigy jar. *d*) Shallow bowl. *e*) Bird effigy. *b, c, d,* and *e* by special permission of Peabody Museum of Harvard University.

147 Plates. *a-f,* averaging about 12 in. across, by special permission of Peabody Museum of Harvard University.

148 Various shapes from various cultures. *a*) Polychrome bowl, Ometepec Island, Managua, Nicaragua. Frizell Coll. Ph: CIW. *b*) Pedestal for large bowl, Colombia. MVBS. *c*) Jaguar tripod in polychrome alligator ware, Chiriqui, Panama. 14½ in. Peabody Museum of Yale University. *d*) Human effigy, Costa Rica. Museo Nacional, San José, Costa Rica. *e*) Effigy with canoe-shaped head, Venezuela. Dr. R. Requeña Coll., N. Y. *f*) Four-footed alligator-ware vessel with two female figures, Chiriqui, Panama. 14¾ in. Zeltner Coll., Peabody Museum of Yale University.

149 *a*) Tripod with monkey figures, Chiriqui, Panama. About 5 in. FM. *b*) Clay stool, Panama. 10¼ in. Peabody Museum of Yale University. *c*) Tripod with monkeys, Costa Rica. 6½ in. MARI. *d*) Bottle with animal decoration, Santarem, Brazil. 7 in. UMP.

150 *a*) Mortuary urn, Ocaña district, Colombia. 26 in. AMNH. *b*) Negative-

# CATALOGUE OF ILLUSTRATIONS

painted vessel with three spouts, Antioquia, Colombia. Quimbaya culture. UMP. *c*) Alligator-ware burial jar, Marajo Island, Brazil. 2 ft. UMP. *d*) Alligator-ware cylindrical vase, Marajo Island. 18 in. UMP.

151 Small pottery heads, from 3 to 5½ in. *a*) Venezuela, Dr. R. Requeña Coll., N. Y. *b, c, d, f,* and *g*) Esmeraldas, Ecuador. Dr. E. Franco Coll., N. Y. *e*) La Tolita, Esmeraldas. MAI. *h*) Esmeraldas. Property of Dr. E. Franco on loan to Brooklyn M.

### ANDEAN AREA

152 Mochica stirrup-spout vessels. *a*) The Trumpeter. 8½ in. UMP. *b*) Warrior on a raft propelled by swimmers. 10⅛ in. UMP.

153 Mochica vessels with story-telling decoration. *a*) Warrior and battle scene, Trujillo, Peru. 9¾ in. After Schmidt. *b*) Bowl with flaring mouth, warriors and captives, Chimbote. Diameter, 15 in. After Schmidt. *c*) Stirrup jar, building with dancers, Chicama. British M. *d*) Stirrup jar with warrior and serpent. 11¾ in. MH.

154 Mochica effigy vessels showing striking poses. *a*) Listening, Trujillo, Peru. MAI. *b*) Sleeping. 9¾ in. UMP. *c*) Smiling, Lambayeque. About 12½ in. MH. *d*) Praying. 7¾ in. After Schmidt.

155 Scenes of Chimu life, black ware. *a*) Double whistle jar, group with hammock. 8 in. long and 10 high. MH. *b*) Double whistle jar, man with llama?, Chan-Chan, Peru. MAI. *c*) Man and children, Lambayeque. MAI. *d*) Whistle jar, man playing the panpipes. 11¾ in. MH.

156 Water jars with animal subjects. *a* and *b*) Chimu, gray with metallic sheen, with monkeys as decoration. 7¼ and 7¾ in. respectively. FM. *c*) Chimu black ware with monkey and birds as decoration. 8⅞ in. Cranbrook Academy of Art, Bloomfield, Mich. *d*) Mochica painted vessel, llama and rider. 8½ in. AMNH. *e*) Mochica double jar in parrot shape, near

Trujillo, Peru. About 9 in. After Schmidt.

157 Animal representations, Peru and Ecuador. *a*) Mochica stirrup jar, striped cat. Worcester Art Museum. *b*) Small dog?, near Cuenca, Ecuador. MH. *c*) Chimu fish, Chimbote, Peru. MAI. *d*) Mochica fragment with puma head, Chicama. 4½ in. After Lehmann and Doering.

158 *a*) Mochica Potato Mother. 10⅛ in. UMP. *b*) Chimu black-ware double jar with pressed relief. AMNH. *c*) Chimu? gourd?, Trujillo, Peru. 6½ in. MARI. *d*) Chimu? black-ware fruit?, Quilea, Peru. MH.

159 Mochica portrait vessels. *a*) About 12 in. PM. *b*) Trujillo, Peru. About 5 in. After Lehmann and Doering.

160 Mochica portrait vessels. *a*) 7¼ in. UMP. *b*) Chicama, Peru. About 8½ in. After Lehmann and Doering.

161 *a*) Mochica effigy jar, with plastic, painted, and incised decoration. BG. *b*) Nazca polychrome effigy of a woman. 7¾ in. MH. *c*) Nazca polychrome effigy of a laughing man. PM. *d*) Mochica effigies, depicting ravages of disease. About 7¼ in. FM.

162 Various shapes from South Coast of Peru and Chile. *a*) Bevel lip bowl, Chincha Valley, Peru. UCAL. *b*) Mug, Sacna, Chile. Atacameña culture. AMNH. *c*) Ica keg-shaped vessel with animal handles. 7 in. After Schmidt. *d* and *e*) Nazca painted vessels, plant and human figures, Chincha Valley. UCAL. *f*) Polychrome painted vase, "cats and mice," Nazca Valley, Peru. FM.

163 Painted ware. *a*) Coast Tiahuanaco vessel with condor and human head. 4 in. *b*) Nazca plates with fish designs. *c*) Coast Tiahuanaco jar with double-serpent figure. About 7 in. *d*) Nazca double-spout jug with fish. 10 in. All MARI.

164 *a*) Coast Tiahuanaco painted jar with handles and figural decoration. 12⅜ in. MAI. *b* and *c*) Nazca beaker shapes with painted decoration. AMNH. *d*) Beaker shape with painted decoration. MAI.

# Weaving

each 6¾ in. PM. c) Section of wide embroidered garment, Nazca. AMNH.

177 a) Embroidered Paracas mantle, double fish design. 10 ft. long and more than 5 ft. wide. Brooklyn M. b) Corner of embroidered Paracas mantle, each figure about 7 in. JW.

178 Coast Tiahuanaco tapestry. a) Poncho. 45 x 41 in. MAI. b) Detail of a wool band, nearly 4 ft. long, each figure 6½ in. long and about 5 high. TM. c) Section of Late Coast Tiahuanaco? garment, wool on cotton warp in Kelim technique. TM.

179 Tapestry. a) Chimu? fish, wool, Kelim technique. 21 x 9 in. TM. b) Ica wool square with figures from Nazca Valley, using Kelim, eccentric, figure-8 techniques. About 18 in. UCAL. c) Coast Tiahuanaco panel with condor, wool on cotton warp. JW.

180 Bags, or pouches. a) Inca? loom-pattern or warp-pattern rep. 8½ x 7 in. TM. b) Late Coast Tiahuanaco bag with embroidered decoration and needle-knitted edges. JW. c) Coast Tiahuanaco tapestry bag with plaited cord top. JW.

181 a) Fragment of Ica? brocade garment with Kelim tapestry border. UMP. b) Ica single-faced wool brocade on cotton crêpe from Nazca Valley. 39 x 28 in. UCAL.

182 Painted plain-woven cotton cloth. a) Chimu? poncho. JW. b) Kitten design, each figure about 4 in. Coast Tiahuanaco?. TM. c) Portion of Late Coast Tiahuanaco? cloth, cats and condors, each square less than 1 in. JW.

183 a) Nazca painted cotton cloth, each bird about 1½ in., Trancas, Nazca Valley, Peru. UCAL. b) Chimu? hairnet of maguey fiber, square-meshed netting, embroidered. AMNH. c) Chimu? square-

meshed lacelike gauze, embroidered. Figure about 4½ in. TM.

184 a) Nazca cotton gauze. UCAL. b) Chimu? gauze with plain bands and openwork, Quintay, Peru. UMP. c) Ica? openwork and plain weave with tapestry border. FM.

185 a) Cotton poncho in weft-loop weave. AMNH. b) Openwork tapestry, cotton warp and wool weft, with spaced warps and tassels. MH. c) Polychrome tapestry with tasseled rosettes. MH. All Chimu?.

186 Two Coast Tiahuanaco wool plush hats. About 6 in. JW.

187 Section of embroidered wool Paracas shawl. Entire piece, 46 x 20 in. TM.

188 a) Paracas mantle of cotton and vicuña wool, with border in three-dimensional knitting. 54 x 21 in. Brooklyn M. b) Detail of border, about 3½ in. wide.

189 a) Ica? poncho, spaced-warp tapestry, Ancon, Peru. USNM. b) Chimu? poncho with applied tapestry medallions, Pachacamac. MVVA. c) Chimu? poncho, plain and open weave, with tassels and applied medallions, Huaco, northern Peru. 37 in. long. PM.

190 Ponchos. a) Late Coast Tiahuanaco? plain weave with embroidered borders and fringe. JW. b) Paracas fringed garment with embroidered and woven bands. 50 x 38 in. AMNH.

191 Inca tapestry ponchos. a) FM. b, c, and d) Island in Lake Titicaca, Bolivia. AMNH.

192 a) Spanish colonial wool tapestry, Peru, 17-18th century. About 8 x 6 ft. MFA. b) Post-Columbian tapestry poncho, island in Lake Titicaca, Bolivia, probably late 16th century. AMNH.

# Metal – Work

204 Inca human and animal figurines. *a*) Alpaca of hammered silver. 12 in. AMNH. *b*) Man, woman, and llama of cast silver. Llama, about 9 in. AMNH. *c*) Copper llama and rider. Cuzco, Peru. 4¼ in. USNM. *d*) Alpaca or guanaco, cast silver alloy with gold head, near Cuzco. 4½ in. FM.

205 Inca bronze knives. *a*) With snake and gold pelican. 5½ in. UMP. *b*) Man and llama. British M. *c*) Boy fishing, Machu Picchu, Peru. 5 in. Peabody Museum of Yale University.

206 Inca implements. *a*) Bronze knife with inlaid handle shaped into a llama head. About 6¼ in. DO. *b*) Bronze "spoon" with bird. 2⅝ in. DO. *c*) Bronze tool with parrot and monkey, said to have been found in El Salvador. 2¾ in. Priv. Coll. *d*) Copper awl or pin with rattle handle and human figures. Inca or Chimu. British M. *e*) Bronze adze in the shape of a bird with copper and silver inlay. 3⅝ in. DO.

207 *a*) Gold scrapers of cosmetic oils (upper left), about 3½ in. Gold disks and necklace, Chavin style. BG. *b*) Chimu gold plates and stirrup jar, Huarmey Valley, Central Coast of Peru. Plates, about 8 in. in diameter; jar, 10½ in. high. AMNH.

208 *a*) Gold disk thought to be a calendar, Peruvian highlands. Diameter, 5¼ in. Chavin and Tiahuanaco characteristics. MAI. *b*) Inca? silver ornaments, Cuzco. Oval, 4⅞ in. MAI. *c* and *d*) Gold disks found near Zacualpa, Guatemala. 5 and 3¼ in. respectively. RC.

209 Gold animal representations of late cultures. *a*) Chimu? beard-tongs with monkeys. About 2½ in. After Lehmann and Doering. *b*) Chimu? earplug with monkeys. Diameter, about 2 in. Schoeller Coll., N. Y. *c*) Face of Ica earplug with colibris. Diameter, 1¾ in. After Lehmann and Doering. *d*) Coast Tiahuanaco? pendant with bird and alligator. British M.

### INTERLYING AREA

210 *a*) Gold breast ornament with Bat-god figure. La Tola Island, Esmeraldas, Ecuador. Diameter, 9½ in. UMP. *b*) Bronze mask, low tin alloy, Esmeraldas. 7½ in. Dr. E. Franco Coll., N. Y. *c*) Bronze disk with puma head, Manabí district. Diameter, 13½ in. British M.

211 *a*) Gold breastplate with Bat-god, excavated among contents of large earthenware chest, La Tola Island, Esmeraldas, Ecuador. 13½ in. wide. UMP. *b*) Small gold mask, Ecuador. About 4 in. British M.

212 Gold breastplate, excavated as 211*a*, La Tola Island, Esmeraldas, Ecuador. 14 in. wide. UMP.

213 *a*) Chibcha gold ornaments, Colombia. Tallest, 5 in. AMNH. *b*) Gold bells, Colombia. Taller, 2½ in. UMP. *c*) Gold anthropomorphic figure, La Guaira, Venezuela. About 5½ in. Dr. R. Requeña Coll., N. Y. *b* and *c* are somewhat suggestive of the Santa Marta style.

214 Quimbaya gold flasks, Antioquia, Colombia. *a*) 7½ in. Brooklyn M. *b*) Museo Arqueológico Nacional, Madrid. *c*) Smaller, about 4 in. British M.

215 *a*) Quimbaya gold pendant blending human and bird elements, Colombia. About 3 in. Cleveland Museum of Art. *b* and *c*) Gold nose ornaments, near Ayapel, Antioquia. About 4 and 4¼ in. wide respectively. UMP.

216 Metamorphosis of a Quimbaya figure, Colombia. *a*) Gold breast ornament with anthropomorphic figure. 2½ in. MFA. *b*) "Gothic" gold breast ornament, Sinu River, northwestern Colombia. About 10 in. MAI. *c*) Three gold breast ornaments. Tallest, about 10½ in. MAI.

217 Versions of knife-shaped pendants, Colombia. *a*) Alloy of gold, silver, and copper, plated with gold, Popayan. About 11 in. Copyright, British M. *b*) Gold. Dept. of Popayan. 4⅛ in. MAI. *c*) Gold, near Quibdo, near Antioquia. 4¾ in. MAI.

218 *a*) Gold plaque with human figures, Colombia, sent to World's Columbian Exposition, Chicago, 1892. *b*) Quimbaya gold

plaque representing a tower with four birds of prey. 6 in. TM. *c* and *d*) Quimbaya cast gold female idols, Antioquia. 6 and 9 in. respectively. PM and UMP.

219 Cast gold staff heads, Colombia. *a*) Quimbaya?, cast in several pieces. 5 in. MFA. *b*) Monteria, Dept. of Bolívar, northwestern Colombia. About 8 in. long. MAI. *c*) Quimbaya? dog, about 2 in., and man blowing trumpet. Museo Preistorico ed Etnografico, Rome.

220 *a*) Quimbaya gold crown with soaring condor, Antioquia, Colombia. 6 in., including bird. UMP. *b*) Quimbaya gold helmet with human figure in repoussé. British M.

221 *a*) Gold helmet, Darien, Panama. 4¾ in., weight 11 oz. PM. *b*) Gold helmet, Sitio Conte, Coclé, Panama. Weight 7⅞ oz. PM.

222 *a*) Gold alligator or crocodile with human prey, Costa Rica. 4¼ in., weight 61½ grams. Museo Nacional, San José, Costa Rica. *b*) Gold shark pendant. Walters Art Gallery, Baltimore. *c*) Massive gold alligator carrying conventionalized object, Coclé, Panama. 7 in. long. TM. *d*) Twin alligators with conventionalized objects, Coclé, Panama. About 3½ in. PM.

223 Embossed gold plaques, Coclé, Panama. *a*) Diameter, 8 in. *b*) About 8½ in. UMP.

224 Masterpieces of the jeweler's art, Coclé, Panama. *a*) Insect of gold and quartz. 2 in. PM. *b*) Gold cuff with animals in repoussé. About 7 in. long. PM. *c*) Gold dogs or alligator cubs. About 2½ in. long. PM. *d*) Solid gold pendant with inset emerald, fashioned into a fantastic animal. 4¼ in. long. UMP.

225 Pendants with twin figures. *a*) *Tumbaga* (alloy of gold and copper), Coclé, Panama. About 3½ in. high and 5 wide. PM. *b*) Gold, Chiriqui?. About 4 in. wide. British M. *c*) Gold, Costa Rica. AMNH.

226 *a*) Gold bird pendant, Costa Rica. About 4 in. MFA. *b*) Gold bird pendant, Colombia. MAI. *c*) Gold figurine with pipe?, Panama. Peabody Museum of Yale

University. *d*) Gold rattle in human form, near volcano of Quarialba, Costa Rica. 3 in. MAI.

### MAYA AND MEXICAN AREAS

227 *a*) Tarascan copper mask of Xipe-Totec. About 5½ in. MN. *b*) Copper bell in form of human face, Honduras. Over 3 in. MARI. *c*) Copper bell in form of turkey, Santa Barbara, British Honduras. About 3 in. PM.

228 Finger rings. *a*) Cast gold with descending eagle and pendant, Oaxaca, Mexico. About 2½ in. long. Oaxaca M. Ph: INAH. *b*) Copper with human head, Guatemala-Salvador border. About 1¼ in. Dr. E. O. Salazar Coll., San Salvador. *c*) Gold with feathered serpent, Oaxaca. About 1 in. MAI. *d*) Gold with glyphs, Oaxaca. Diameter, about ⅞ in. MN. *e*) Gold with feathered serpent, Oaxaca. About 1 in. UMP.

229 Gold articles of personal adornment, Oaxaca, Mexico. *a*) Labret, or lipplug, Ejutla. About 2½ in. long, including tongue. MAI. *b*) Gold diadem, diameter 6 in., and repoussé feather, about 13½ in., Monte Alban. Oaxaca M. Ph: INAH. *c*) Labret, Tlacolula. AMNH. *d*) Bracelet, Tomb 7, Monte Alban. Oaxaca M. Ph: Osuna.

230 Necklaces. *a*) Gold, Tomb 7, Monte Alban, Oaxaca, Mexico. About 2½ in. wide. Oaxaca M. Ph: INAH. *b*) Toltec silver and copper alloy, Texcoco, Mexico. FM. *c*) Gold, Tomb 7, Monte Alban. Oaxaca M. Ph: Osuna.

231 *a*) Mixtec cast gold pectoral of Jaguar Knight as God of Death, Tomb 7, Monte Alban, Oaxaca, Mexico. 4½ in., weight 3 oz. Oaxaca M. Ph: Osuna. *b*) Gold figure of the Aztec king, Tizoc, Texcoco, Mexico. 3½ in. MAI. *c*) Cast gold pectoral with fantastic animal, Costa Rica. AMNH.

232 *a*) Gold pendant made up of seven elements. 8½ in. long. *b*) Small gold mask of Xipe-Totec. 2¾ in. Both from Tomb 7, Monte Alban, Oaxaca, Mexico, and in Oaxaca M. Phs: Osuna.

# METAL-WORK

# Jade and Other Semiprecious Stones

Ph: EZK. By special permission of Carnegie Institution of Washington. *d*) Green diorite, Mexico. About 3 in. BG.

243 *a*) Totonac serpentine statuette, Vera Cruz, Mexico. 4¼ in. FM. *b*) Tiger-mouth figure, Puebla, Mexico. AMNH. *c*) Olmec type. 4 in. BG. *d*) Olmec type. Priv. Coll.

244 *a*) Crystal bead necklace, Chichen Itzá, Yucatan, Mexico. FM. *b*) Fragment of carved jade disk, Chichen Itzá. PM. *c*) Jade necklace and pendant. Length of pendant, 2¼ in. UMP.

245 Small pendants in the form of human heads, ranging from 2½ to 3½ in. and showing stylistic variations. *a*) Mexico. JW. *b*) Mexico. AMNH. *c*) Mexico. JW. *d*) Mexico. Priv. Coll. *e*) Palenque, Chiapas, Mexico. MAI. *f*) Mexico. UMP. *g*) El Salvador. Zanotti Coll., El Salvador. Ph: EZK. *h*) Yucatan, Mexico. MARI.

246 *a*) Olmec pectoral. 3¼ in. British M. *b*) Olmec plaque. 6 in. MN. Both Mexico.

247 Small heads, Mexico. *a*) Pierre Matisse Gallery, N. Y. *b*) 1¾ in. BG. *c*) About 2½ in. BG. *d*) Less than 3 in. Harold L. Wallace Coll., Ann Arbor, Mich.

248 Large stone masks. *a*) Aztec jade representation of Coyolaxhqui, Vera Cruz?. About 4½ in. PM. *b*) Dark green stone. About 4½ in. Totonac? with Olmec traits. PM. *c*) Totonac. Vera Cruz. 7⅛ in. PM. *d*) Totonac jade. 5 in. MN.

249 Large stone masks. *a* and *d*) Toltec. About 10 in. MN. *b*) Showing Toltec influence. BG. *c*) Of indefinite style. About 9 in. MVVA.

250 *a*) Black stone mask of Xipe-Totec, Oaxaca, Mexico. 4¼ in. MH. *b*) Round jade mask, probably unfinished. 3¾ in. DO. *c*) Toltec mask. 4¾ in. DO. *d*) Large green serpentine mask. 18 in. Priv. Coll.

251 *a*) Jaguar head, Piedras Negras, Guatemala. About 3 in. On loan from the Govt. of Guatemala to UMP. *b*) Ob-

sidian monkey head, Puebla, Mexico. 4 in. MVVA. *c*) Small mask with inlaid eyes, Achapuan, El Salvador. About 2 in. Zanotti Coll., El Salvador. Ph: EZK. *d*) Amphibian, provenience unknown. About 3 in. BG. *e*) Fan handle, Tomb 7, Monte Alban, Oaxaca, Mexico. About 5 in. Oaxaca M. Ph: INAH. *f*) Hand-shaped pendant, Ulua Valley, Honduras. 1½ in. MARI.

252 Standing human figures. *a*) Puebla, Mexico. 20 in. Puebla M. Ph: EZK. *b*) Provenience unknown. About 5 in. Priv. Coll. *c* and *d*) Statuette with Olmec traits. Provenience unknown. About 9½ in. DO.

253 Seated human figures. *a*) Dark stone, provenience unknown. Under 4 in. BG. *b*) Pyrite with Olmec tendencies, provenience unknown. Wadsworth Atheneum, Hartford, Conn. *c*) Dark jade, found near La Lima, near Ulua Valley, Honduras. About 3½ in. Property of Doris Stone, New Orleans. Ph: Roy Trahan. MARI. *d*) Light green jade with Olmec traits, provenience unknown. 4¼ in. Cleveland Museum of Art.

254 *a*) Vessel representing Tlaloc, Mexican Rain-god, Mexico. 8¾ in., weight 10 lbs. 3 oz. MN. *b*) Wernerite statue of Toci, Mother of the Gods, Mexico. 7½ in. BG.

255 Rock-crystal objects. *a*) Goblet, Tomb 7, Monte Alban, Oaxaca, Mexico. About 4½ in. high and 3 in diameter. Oaxaca M. Ph: Osuna. *b*) Life-size skull, Mexico. British M.

256 *a*) Life-size rock-crystal frog, Mexico. BG. *b*) Rock-crystal man in the moon, Mexico. MH. *c*) Obsidian model of a temple-base, found near Puebla, Mexico. 8 in. Puebla M. Ph: EZK. *d*) Maya? eccentric flint in human shape. About 7½ in. high and less than ¼ in. thick. BG.

257 *a*) Vase of Mexican onyx, Tomb 7, Monte Alban, Oaxaca, Mexico. Oaxaca M. Ph: Osuna. *b*) Small jade vase, El Salvador. About 2 in. Priv. Coll. Ph: EZK. *c* and *d*) Two Totonac onyx vases, Isla de

# Murals and Manuscripts

# CATALOGUE OF ILLUSTRATIONS

# Miscellaneous Applied Arts

# Facets of Daily Life

# CATALOGUE OF ILLUSTRATIONS

PLATE

UMP. *b*) Pottery incense burner using human figure for decoration, San Lorenzo, Oaxaca, Mexico. 12¼ in. long. MAI. *c*) Pottery effigy pipe in human shape, Oaxaca. View of back. 6⅜ in. long. MAI.

### MIRRORS

298 *a*) Obsidian mirror with gilded wood frame, Vera Cruz?, Mexico. Diameter, about 10 in. AMNH. *b*) Chimu? pyrite mirror with carved and painted wood frame, coast of Peru. Over-all length, 9¼ in. MAI. *c*) Carved and painted wood back of a Chimu mirror, Lambayeque, Peru. 9½ in. with handle. MAI.

### COUNTING AND MEASURING

299 *a*) Chimu balance scale with beam of carved bone and netted bags, Peru. British M. *b*) *Quipu,* or knot record, Chancay, Peru. AMNH.

### ROADS

300 *a*) Airview of jungle bush revealing the course of two intersecting Maya roads, Yucatan, Mexico. Ph: CIW. *b*) Airview of remnants of Chimu highway and ruin in coastal sands, Chicama Valley, Peru. Ph: Aerial Explorations, Inc., N. Y.

### CITY-PLANNING

301 *a*) Airview of Pueblo ruins, Aztec, New Mexico. Ph: AMNH. *b*) Airview of ancient Maya walled seacoast city, Tulum, Quintana Roo, Mexico. Ph: CIW.

302 *a*) Airview of the Citadel, with Quetzal-

PLATE

coatl Temple, Teotihuacan, Mexico. Ph: Pan American Airways System. *b*) Airview of a section of the ancient Chimu capital, Chan-Chan, Peru. Ph: Aerial Explorations, Inc., N. Y.

### BATHS AND RESERVOIRS

303 *a*) Partly restored antechamber and entrance to Maya sweat bath, Chichen Itzá, Yucatan, Mexico. Ph: CIW. *b*) Restored section of same showing vapor vent. Ph: CIW. *c*) Ruins of an Inca reservoir and water-distributing system, Sacsahuaman, Peru. Ph: Serge A. Korff.

### STAIRWAYS

304 Stairway to main entrance, El Castillo, Chichen Itzá, Yucatan, Mexico. Ph: copyright, Laura Gilpin, Colorado Springs. Inset: Wooden beam with hewn footholds, a primitive ladder still in use, Guatemala-Salvador border. Ph: EZK.

305 *a*) Ruined east stairway, before restoration, Temple of the Dwarf, Uxmal, Yucatan, Mexico. Ph: Pan American Airways System. *b*) Stairway connecting different levels, Machu Picchu, Peru. Ph: Grace Line.

### ENVOI

306 Phuyu Pata Marka, Peru, the City above the Clouds, near Machu Picchu. *a*) View from the northeast, showing water channels and basins in foreground. *b*) View from the northwest. Excavated and photographed by Paul Fejös of the Viking Fund. Inc.

# REGISTER OF MUSEUMS AND COLLECTIONS

# Register of Museums and Collections

This list shows the location of most of the objects illustrated in this survey. In addition, there are twenty-five private collections represented which are not included here.

American Museum of Natural History, New York, N.Y.
28b, 33d, 62a, 69b, 89a, 97c, 98b, 101b, 104c, 114b, 115c, 115d, 117a, 118a, 118c, 119a, 134a, 140b, 142d, 150a, 156d, 158b, 162b, 164b, 164c, 165a, 166a, 166b, 167a, 169c, 171c, 172b, 176c, 183b, 185a, 190b, 191b, 191c, 191d, 192b, 196a, 204a, 204b, 207b, 213a, 225c, 229c, 231c, 243b, 245b, 276a, 276e, 289c, 293a, 294a, 294c, 294d, 294f, 296c, 298a, 299b.

British Museum, London, England
59a, 61a, 76b, 85b, 86a, 90, 111c, 117c, 126c, 131a, 144a, 153c, 174a, 174b, 203b, 205b, 206d, 209d, 210c, 211b, 214c, 217a, 220b, 225b, 238b, 242b, 246a, 255b, 275a, 278a, 278b, 278c, 279a, 292d, 299a.

Brooklyn Museum, Brooklyn, N.Y.
27b, 30b, 63b, 146a, 151h, 177a, 188a, 214a.

Brummer Gallery, New York, N.Y.
61b, 68c, 68d, 88c, 94a, 95b, 115a, 116c, 117e, 125a, 131d, 137a, 161a, 207a, 235b, 237c, 237d, 239f, 240b, 241g, 242d, 243c, 247b, 247c, 249b, 251d, 253a, 254b, 256a, 256d, 276c, 282b.

Buffalo Fine Arts Academy, Albright Art Gallery, Buffalo, N.Y.
135a.

Buffalo Museum of Science, Buffalo, N.Y.
106e.

Carnegie Institution of Washington, Washington, D.C.
262a, 263a.

City Art Museum, St. Louis, Mo.
132a.

Cleveland Museum of Art, Cleveland, Ohio
117b, 195c, 215a, 253d.

Copan Museum, Copan, Honduras
82a, 83b.

Cranbrook Academy of Art, Bloomfield, Mich.
66a, 156c, 199a, 202a.

Dartmouth College Museum, Hanover, N.H.
88b.

Denver Art Museum, Denver, Colo.
102b.

Dumbarton Oaks Collection, Washington, D.C.
66b, 206a, 206b, 206e, 241a, 250b, 250c, 252c, 252d.

Field Museum, Chicago, Ill.
108b, 109c, 111a, 111d, 111e, 112b, 114a, 114c, 125b, 126a, 133b, 149a, 156a, 156b, 161d, 162f, 184c, 191a, 193a, 193b, 200a, 204d, 230b, 243a, 244a, 258a, 272a, 276d, 277a, 282c, 296f.

Institute of Arts, Minneapolis, Minn.
64a.

Instituto Nacional de Antropología e Historia, Mexico, D.F.
264d.

Laboratory of Anthropology, Santa Fé, N.M.
101c, 102c, 103c, 105a, 105d.

Los Angeles Museum of History, Science, and Art, Los Angeles, Calif.
101e, 145c, 282a, 285a.

Metropolitan Museum of Art, New York, N.Y.
63b, 114b.

Middle American Research Institute, Tulane University, New Orleans, La.
60b, 80d, 86d, 94b, 116d, 126b, 134d, 134e, 140a, 142e, 143a, 145b, 149c, 158c, 163a, 163b, 163c, 163d, 227b, 237a, 245h, 251f, 281b.

Montezuma Castle National Museum, Montezuma Castle, Ariz.
171a.

Musée de l'Homme, Paris, France
113c, 123b, 133a, 133c, 153d, 154c, 155a, 155d, 157b, 158d, 161b, 185b, 185c, 200b, 238a, 250a, 256b.

Museo Arqueológico, Guatemala, Guatemala
72a, 97a, 97b, 127a, 127b, 127c, 127d, 128a, 128b, 128c, 129a, 132b, 134b, 135c, 136a, 136c, 141a, 141d, 145d, 236b, 242c.

Museo Arqueológico Nacional, Madrid, Spain
81a, 214b.

Museo de la Universidad, Lima, Peru
99a.

Museo Nacional, San José, Costa Rica
97d, 148d, 222a, 294e.

Museo Nacional de Arqueología, Lima, Peru
99b, 198a, 198c, 199c, 201a, 202c, 258c.

Museo Nacional de Arqueología, Historia y Etnografia, Mexico, D.F.
58a, 58b, 65a, 65c, 67a, 67b, 67c, 69a, 75b, 78b, 82b, 82c, 84b, 93b, 110a, 110b, 110c, 111b, 111f, 112c, 113a, 115b, 119b, 121c, 122a, 122b, 124a, 124b, 227a, 228d, 233b, 234a, 237f, 241f, 246b, 248d, 249a, 249d, 254a, 257c, 257d, 260a, 260b, 261b, 269, 285b, 285c, 287a, 292a, 292b, 292e, 293c.

Museo Preistorico ed Etnografico, Rome, Italy
219c, 273a.

Museum für Völkerkunde, Basle, Switzerland
148b, 274.

Museum für Völkerkunde, Berlin, Germany
121a, 131b, 273c.

Museum für Völkerkunde, Vienna, Austria
59b, 65b, 68b, 189b, 239b, 240a, 249c, 251b, 286a, 287b, 287c.

Museum of Art, Providence, R.I.
201b.

Museum of Fine Arts, Boston, Mass.
192a, 202b, 216a, 219a, 226a.

Museum of New Mexico, Santa Fé, N.M.
4b, 170a.

Museum of the American Indian, Heye Foundation, New York, N.Y.
86c, 101a, 103f, 108c, 108d, 109b, 109d, 114d, 117d, 123a, 123c, 125c, 133d, 138a, 139d, 143c, 144c, 151e, 154a, 155b, 155c, 157c, 164a, 164d, 178a, 194a, 194b, 194c, 195b, 195d, 197a, 198b, 199b, 200c, 208a, 208b, 216b, 216c, 217b, 217c, 219b, 226b, 226d, 228c, 229a, 231b, 233a, 240c, 240d, 241b, 242a, 245e, 258b, 271a, 272b, 279b, 280a, 280b, 280c, 283a, 283b, 283c, 289a, 289b, 295a, 296e, 297b, 297c, 298b, 298c.

Oaxaca Museum, Oaxaca, Mexico
68a, 123d, 124c, 228a, 229b, 229d, 230a, 230c, 231a, 232a, 232b, 251e, 255a, 257a, 284b, 284c.

Ohio State Museum, Columbus, Ohio
194d, 295b, 295d, 296a, 296b, 296d.

Peabody Museum of Harvard University, Cambridge, Mass.
77a, 78a, 85a, 87, 88d, 89b, 102a, 106a, 106c, 106e, 107, 108a, 109a, 134c, 137b, 142c, 146b, 146c, 146d, 146e, 147a, 147b, 147c, 147d, 147e, 147f, 159a, 161c, 171b, 176b, 189c, 197b, 218c, 221a, 221b, 222d, 224a, 224b, 224c, 225a, 227c, 234b, 238c, 238d, 240e, 240f, 241d, 244b, 248a, 248b, 248c, 259a, 259b, 262b, 263c, 273b, 276f, 284a.

Peabody Museum of Yale University, New Haven, Conn.
148c, 148f, 149b, 205c, 226c, 295c.

Phillips Academy, Andover, Mass.
281a, 281c.

Pitti Gallery, Florence, Italy
288.

Puebla Museum, Puebla, Mexico
59c, 60c, 252a, 256c, 293b.

Rijks Museum, Leyden, Holland
235a.

Rossbach Collection, Chichicastenango, Guatemala
96a, 136b, 141b, 141c, 208c, 208d, 237e, 241c, 241h.

Southwest Museum, Los Angeles, Calif.
170b.